Protecting Student Data Privacy

Protecting Student Data Privacy

Classroom Fundamentals

Linnette Attai

ROWMAN & LITTLEFIELD
Lanham • Boulder • New York • London

Published by Rowman & Littlefield
An imprint of The Rowman & Littlefield Publishing Group, Inc.
4501 Forbes Boulevard, Suite 200, Lanham, Maryland 20706
www.rowman.com

6 Tinworth Street, London SE11 5AL, United Kingdom

British Library Cataloguing in Publication Information Available

Library of Congress Cataloging-in-Publication Data

Names: Attai, Linnette J., author.
Title: Protecting student data privacy : classroom fundamentals / Linnette Attai.
Description: Lanham : Rowman & Littlefield, [2019] | Includes bibliographical
   references. | Summary: "Teachers handle student data every day, but too often
   they are not provided with the guidance they need to protect student data privacy"
   — Provided by publisher.
Identifiers: LCCN 2019005456 (print) | LCCN 2019022367 (ebook) | ISBN
   9781475845211 (cloth : alk. paper) | ISBN 9781475845228 (pbk. : alk. paper)
Subjects: LCSH: Student records. | Privacy, Right of.
Classification: LCC LB2845.7 .A878 2019 (print) | LCC LB2845.7 (ebook) | DDC
   371.2/1—dc23
LC record available at https://lccn.loc.gov/2019005456
LC ebook record available at https://lccn.loc.gov/2019022367

♾™ The paper used in this publication meets the minimum requirements of American National Standard for Information Sciences—Permanence of Paper for Printed Library Materials, ANSI/NISO Z39.48-1992.

For my teachers, Pam, Maureen, and David

Contents

Introduction

As a teacher, you play a critical role in protecting the privacy of your students' personal information, ensuring that your educational institution remains compliant with student data privacy laws, and addressing parent questions about your use of technology in the classroom. After all, you handle student data every day, and very few individuals in your organization have the same depth and breadth of access to student data for the variety of uses as you do.

However, most of you have not been provided with properly tailored training—or, in many cases, *any* training—to be able to meet those responsibilities, or even to understand fully how the technology you choose to use in the classroom operates with respect to collection and protection of student data.

Yet community members, parent advocates, legislators, and even some in your educational institution seem to have an expectation that you will, without any dedicated training, understand how to protect student data privacy. That you don't require guidance to translate the laws and policies into action, or in some cases, that perhaps simply the act of bringing technology into the classroom, or the knowledge that your educational institution no longer uses pencil and paper as its fundamental media for record keeping, will render you as an educator with a detailed understanding and appreciation for your role and responsibility in protecting the privacy of student data.

This likely won't be the first time you've heard that you have a role to play in protecting student data privacy, and that it is important work. Maybe your technology team has been telling you to create complex passwords, lock your devices, and not keep your passwords on a note stuck on your computer. Perhaps your technology director has restricted your access to certain data or has given you instructions about where to store and not store student data. Or perhaps every time you bring a new piece of technology into the classroom,

your technology team insists that it could disrupt the network or run afoul of
your institution's privacy policies.

You also may have received a variety of policies to read covering this
topic, adding to your existing pile of documents to review and absorb.

Despite best intentions, sometimes missing from these encounters is the
why and the how of protecting student data privacy. Why is it important?
Among all of the responsibilities on your plate, why does this one matter?
And if it does matter, how should you act? How can you protect the privacy
of student data without wholly disrupting your established work style and lofty
goals for supporting student success, becoming an expert in privacy laws and
spending vast amounts of free time you don't have to figure it all out?

Of course, more often than not, these questions haven't been answered
because the investment hasn't been made in the necessary training, professional development, and guidance—often with good reason. The additional
resources in the form of knowledge, time, and training materials required to
provide the right guidance are in remarkably short supply in most educational
institutions, and the number of priorities competing for those resources and
for your attention can be overwhelming.

As a teacher, there's no doubt that your priorities are already vast and
complex. From the fundamental, sometimes exhausting work of educating
students, to addressing many of the social and emotional challenges that appear in your classroom every day, it's easy to understand why learning about
student data privacy might take a backseat to other work, or in many cases,
not even make it into the vehicle.

But the truth is that protecting student data privacy is part of the fundamental responsibility of care that you have for your students. As such, learning
what it takes to provide that care is necessary and important. By engaging
in this learning, you will not only understand how to better protect your students' data, but also your own. In addition, you'll be much better positioned
to prepare your students for life in the modern age, instilling within them a
sense that not only does their privacy matter, but they can make conscious
decisions about how they manage the information they may decide to share
with the world in the future.

Learning how to protect student data privacy is not a simple task by any
means, and ultimately it will require you to be open to the idea of making
some small but impactful behavioral changes, including changes in the way
you currently consider your discovery and use of classroom technologies.

Given the enormity of your current responsibilities, it seems almost unfair
to add what might seem like a new responsibility to your repertoire. In an
ideal world, the technology you bring into the classroom would come ready-
made to properly protect your students' privacy; and a simple, one-page man-

ual would provide you with the guidance you need to govern your behavior in order to properly protect your students' data and your own.

Unfortunately, it's not that easy. The truth is that technology came into most educational institutions before the proper foundation had been laid to protect student data. Educational institutions have been trying to catch up to the requirements of privacy and security ever since. Some have made tremendous progress and have robust data protection programs in place, whereas others have just begun.

Regardless of where your institution sits on the readiness spectrum, the role you play in supporting and enhancing that work is critical. The laws are complex; the expectations of legislators, parents, and parent advocates are high; and the risks to your students and your educational institution often are very real. Your help is required in order to create an ecosystem in which your students may flourish using technology without making risky trade-offs in their privacy.

You're not in it alone. A program that protects the privacy of student data requires a holistic approach in which everyone in the organization plays a role. Conversely, if one individual is not playing their role well, the whole system can falter.

However, you've also already proven that you are an agent and a driver of change by bringing technology into the classroom and adapting your style of teaching to encompass different methods and media to best reach your students.

In doing so, you've transformed your classroom, permitting each of your learners to work at their own pace, in their own way. You've reached and engaged your students in unique new ways and now have more information than ever to inform your practice and their education. Embracing change is part of how you stay relevant and fresh for your students and your career.

This is not about restriction, although sometimes it may seem that way. It's about providing you with the knowledge to evolve and improve your privacy behaviors, guiding you to make savvier, more deliberate and more effective decisions about your use of technology and student data.

It is my hope that this book will help you not only better protect the privacy of student data, but also improve your practices in relation to your use of technology and student data.

A lofty goal? Perhaps, but one worth working toward.

Author's Note:

In this book, "educational institution" refers to any school, district, education agency, or any similarly organized entity in which you teach. In addition, although the laws use very different terminology to define information that could be used to identify a student and thus require certain data privacy protections, here we'll simply refer to "student personal information," except when the discussion is centered on a specific law, in which case the legally defined term will be used.

A number of individuals within educational institutions are responsible for managing a technology program. Common titles include chief technology officer, chief information officer, IT director, chief security officer, technology architect, and instructional technology specialist. In some institutions, a team of individuals manages a technology program; in others, a principal or teachers may lead the program.

The roles and organizational structures vary widely and usually depend on financial resources, the institution's needs, and capacity. To simplify and make for a universal construct, this book refers to these individuals as the "technology team," even if your institution has a team of one.

References to "parent" are intended to be inclusive of the legal guardian, and "technology provider" refers to any vendor, contractor, operator, or similar individual or organization that provides technology products and services to an educational institution, including websites, apps, and other internet-connected technologies.

In these pages, you'll also find a number of examples of behavior that might jeopardize the privacy or security of student data. Some you may recognize, but others may seem far-fetched. They're all very real and common actions, gleaned from interviews with numerous teachers, technology teams, and educational institution leadership. They're included not to call attention to the missteps, but to illustrate how simple actions can result in an invasion of privacy and the importance of being thoughtful about data use.

If you do recognize yourself or a colleague in these pages, you should come away from the reading better informed about why and how to adjust those behaviors to better protect your students in the future. You'll also be able to use some of what you learn here to inform how to better manage your own privacy in the way you see fit.

Please note that this is not, and should not be construed as legal or professional advice of any kind, nor is it intended to replace training or policies provided by your educational institution. It is a guide to the fundamentals, intended to help you as an educator better understand why and how to protect student data privacy.

Finally, although this book is primarily geared toward K–12 teachers, the concepts are applicable to teachers at all levels of education, and it is my hope that it will prove useful to anyone working with students.

Chapter One

What Is Data Privacy and Why Does It Matter?

As a teacher, why should you learn about student data privacy? Given everything else on your plate, why should this topic be part of your education and professional development? These are fair questions, especially considering that you already spend a good deal of time juggling the professional development requirements of your state and your educational institution to maintain your accreditation and improve your practices.

It's not uncommon for educators to spend at least 15–20 hours each year, and in some states quite a bit more, in mandatory training[1] covering everything from child maltreatment, active-shooter drills, handling blood-borne pathogens, and, yes, classroom management and subject matter training. That, of course, is in addition to the professional development you undertake on your own to improve your techniques and open your eyes to new approaches to the work. Why yet another topic to unpack and understand?

As a teacher, you make decisions about your students' data privacy every day. Whether deliberately or not, almost everything you do with and for your students involves a decision that may impact their privacy. Some examples include:

- Recording grades;
- Managing an accommodation;
- Developing learning plans;
- Giving a student permission to leave class to visit the nurse;
- Making notes about a student's aptitudes and attitudes;
- Deciding which apps, websites, and other technology products your students will use;

- Speaking to parents about their child's classroom performance;
- Consulting with colleagues for ideas on managing a difficult classroom situation.

Yet, with all of these decisions being made all of the time, many of you are not receiving the education you need to ensure that you construct your decisions in a way that appropriately protects your students.

As a dedicated educator, you take on the enormous responsibility of providing a high standard of care for your students. You go far beyond ensuring that they are educated, and look out for their well-being, often encompassing on some level their mental, social, and emotional care. With all of the hours you spend with your students, you see their triumphs, their struggles, and everything in between. However, more often than not you are left without real guidance on how to care for their personal information, which is simply an extension of their being.

To change that and to empower you with the information you need to properly manage your students' privacy, it is critically important that you learn how to protect their data while still being able to effectively leverage the information you need to support and guide them on their pathways to success.

WHAT DO WE MEAN BY DATA PRIVACY?

Privacy means different things to different people. As a result, it's helpful to define our terms before we delve into the work.

For many parents, when they think about the privacy of student data, especially student data collected by technology providers, their concerns often veer into considerations for the security of their child's information. That is, assurance that bad actors will not hack into a data server and steal their child's information, or that their child's information won't be left exposed for others to see.

Much of that is actually consideration for data security, which is related to privacy but is a distinct discipline. Security practices focus on maintaining the confidentiality, integrity, and availability of the data. A variety of technological tools are available and necessary to help ensure the security of information, the servers on which it is stored, and the networks through which it flows. Firewalls, secure coding practices, multi-factor authentication, patching, and virus scanning are just some of the tools and tactics at our disposal that, when implemented properly, help protect the security of the data.

Security also encompasses physical protections, including locks on doors, and administrative tools, such as rules about password complexity and policies about who may access what data, that often are enforced with the help of technology.

For many parents, a lock on the door of data—literally and figuratively—would be a comfort. If only it were that simple.

All of the technology in the world won't maintain the security of the data. Instead, our behavior is the ingredient that can make or break security. More than any technology, human error is often the culprit in compromising the security of the data.[2] If the technology is not built properly, if we don't configure it properly, if we act in a way that compromises or negates the protections that technology provides, the information is put at risk.

What does it look like to have behavior compromise security? Downloading student data onto an unencrypted laptop, leaving a password next to the computer for convenience, using simple passwords, using the same password for all systems, using public Wi-Fi for work purposes—these are common examples of the human behaviors that have resulted in very challenging data security incidents in educational institutions. Acting in accordance with solid, fundamentally sound privacy principles can do much to help protect the security of the data.

However, it's not just security that concerns parents. Parents often are concerned that, even though you may bring technology into your classroom to serve a specific educational purpose, the technology provider may use their child's data, especially personal information, for reasons unrelated to that educational purpose.

A common question is whether a technology provider is using student data to generate revenue. For example, is the technology provider selling the students' personal information? Is the provider using the data to track students across unrelated sites and services on the internet for the purpose of serving them advertising?

As you may know, legal prohibitions on this type of behavior exist when the technology provider knowingly obtains access to the student data through your educational institution. However, the fear remains real. If you're not choosing technologies that are compliant with the laws—in some cases because the technology simply wasn't intended to be used with students—there is risk.

Yet another common concern for parents is if the data being collected today might adversely impact their child's future. Questions abound about whether it may become a true permanent record.

Unlike in the past, where any semblance of a permanent school record either has been destroyed or still sits in a dusty file cabinet in a school basement, long forgotten and deteriorating with time, today's school record is most commonly in cloud-based storage. Parents often fear that, as a result of that storage, the record will be attached to their child forever and, somehow, will be used against them. A low grade, a behavioral misstep, or any number of other troubles a child might get into when very young, no matter how small or insignificant, might come back to haunt them when they apply to college or enter the workforce.

No evidence may exist that this particular concern will come to fruition, but questions linger about how permanent the permanent record really is, how pervasive it is, and how it might be used.

Young people, on the other hand, are more likely to equate privacy with "personal," and their level of interest and concern with their privacy may vary with the circumstances. For example, a young teen may connect with a parent on a social media platform and keep all of their activity on that site open to their parent. However, if the teen is engaged in a conversation on social media with friends, they may find it intrusive if the parent chimes in on the discussion. To young people, those discussions are meant to be "private" even though they're happening in public.

That's likely one of the reasons why many adults believe that children don't care about their privacy: We perceive that children are willing to share information about themselves with few boundaries. The truth, however, is that what young people mean by privacy and what adults mean by privacy are sometimes very different. For many young people, managing privacy is a complex process of controlling when, where, and how they share personal information and how it will be received by those with whom they share it. In that sense, the definition of privacy takes shape in accordance with the context.[3]

Although it may not seem clear at first glance, the young person's view of privacy is very close to the idea of privacy as we want to discuss it. It considers who may have access to what information, when, and for what purpose. That is also, in part, how student data privacy laws consider data privacy. The privacy protections that need to be in place often depend on the context in which the data is being used or shared.

The laws also consider the sensitivity of the data as fundamental to determining how robustly it should be protected.

The discipline of data privacy is concerned with what data we collect, how we collect it, what we do with it, and how and with whom we share it. It is, first and foremost, about how we act in relation to the data.

As we discuss privacy, we'll consider that a fundamental part of privacy is the right to determine for ourselves when, how, and what of our information we communicate to others. In many cases, when it comes to your students, you are making some of those determinations for them by the way you manage your classroom and the technology you require your students to use. It's just one of the many reasons to ensure that you're equipped with the information you need to make good privacy decisions about their information: you are responsible for both your privacy and theirs.

We can't forget that part of the responsibility for making good privacy decisions for your students is to understand that how each student or their parent may view their privacy can vary widely. Although we can speak in broad strokes about how parents or students might express their privacy concerns, and how they differ from each other, every person has their own ideas about what they consider to be private.

You may not want to discuss your finances with even your closest friend, while your friend may talk endlessly and openly about money concerns. One student might be embarrassed if a friend found out about a grade that another student would consider exceptional. A family member might consider "that story" told at the holiday dinner table to be mortifying, even though everyone else in the family finds it charming and funny.

Our view of privacy may vary depending on what information is being shared, the circumstances in which the information is being shared, with whom the information is being shared, whether the information might be shared beyond the intended recipient, or some combination of these factors.

The point is that each of us has a different idea about what privacy means. Privacy is personal. Therefore, before making a decision about someone else's privacy, as you do with your students, it's important to have the right frameworks in place to help guide and inform you.

When done well, data privacy in schools is managed via complex and rigorous legal frameworks. Those often are articulated in a broad range of policies that set the foundation for behavior. What those policies are depends, at a minimum, on the regulations. When developed properly, however, the policies encompass not only a baseline standard of legal compliance for your educational institution, but also the organization's mission and vision, its ethical boundaries, how the data is intended to be used, and the expectations of the community in which you work.

The policies should provide you with guidance needed to operate in compliance with both the laws and the expectations of the individuals whose data has been collected. In the case of educational institutions, those expectations extend to parents of students under age eighteen or not yet enrolled in a higher education institution. The policies are then accompanied by procedures that explain how to meet the policy requirements.

Your educational institution may or may not have these policies and procedures in place, or they may not yet be as mature and robust as what is suggested here. For many institutions, policy and procedure development is a work in progress. However, even if that's the case, you can still exercise solid, privacy-forward decision-making skills to better protect your students as your institution's policies evolve.

If your educational institution does have a strong privacy program in place with the accompanying policies and procedures, it may surprise you to learn that behind those policies and procedures was likely consideration not just for the rules and restrictions, but also for how student data might best be used to support the students.

Thinking about protecting the privacy of student data, and thus establishing the frameworks for privacy policies should begin by considering not only what you can't do with data, but what you want to, are able to, and *should* do with the data, ethically, to support student success. It is about first establishing how data may be used to support the students' education, then developing the guardrails around it that permit you and your colleagues to make consistent decisions to protect the data in the context of what is legally permissible, ethical, aligned with your unique community norms, and least intrusive to the student.

Bear in mind that the decisions you make about student data privacy impact not only the privacy of your students, but also the legality of your educational institution's operations. Seemingly simple decisions you may make about student data privacy—sharing information with friends about a student who made the day more challenging than usual, peeking at the record of that boy your daughter is dating, deciding to use a new app in the classroom, or copying your lesson plans and grades into a personal file—can all impact your institution's legal standing in relation to both federal and state regulations.

If the task of properly managing student data privacy is beginning to sound daunting, rest assured that you can take simple steps to do it well that will not adversely impact the way you teach or the tools you bring into the classroom to best support your students. It also won't require you to become an expert in technology or in any of the laws.

However, ensuring the privacy of your students' data is most strongly impacted by your behavior. Understanding both the fundamental behaviors that protect privacy and those that adversely impact privacy will allow you to extend the standard of care that you provide to your students to their data, thus helping you to better protect the whole child.

NOTES AND NEXT STEPS

1. What does data privacy mean to you? Does the importance you place on your data privacy vary depending on the circumstances? What do you

expect of your educational institution when it comes to protecting your personal information?

2. What does data privacy mean to your students? How might you leverage their current perspectives on personal privacy to talk to them about their data privacy?

3. What expectations do you think parents in your community have about how you protect their children's data privacy? What do you think they expect in regard to how and why you bring technology into the classroom?

Chapter Two

How Did We Get Here?

How did we get to a place where it became critically important that you learn the ins and outs of student data privacy? In some ways, you always have been mindful of your students' privacy. When you return test papers facedown so that students can't see each other's grades; when you have a quiet conversation with a student after class about their performance or behavior, away from the prying eyes and ears of other students; or when you open your door to students to come in before school for a little extra help, when no other student will be the wiser, you are protecting their privacy and in turn, the privacy of their personal information.

However, with the introduction of technology into the classroom, protecting your students' data privacy became quite a bit more challenging. The sheer variety of information being collected, the companies with which it may be shared, the different combinations of data, and how the laws apply to different use cases for the data makes it impossible to manage based solely on instinct, good intentions, and common sense. It requires exploration, questioning, and deliberate, guided, active decision making governed by your educational institution's policies and processes.

It was education technology that sparked the climate of intense scrutiny and concern about student data privacy that exists today with parents, legislators, and your educational institution's leadership. Looking back at how things unfolded and the sheer speed and volume with which technology was brought into schools, it was predictable that the climate would heat up.

When technology came into the classroom, it turned the environment from something that had been quite well known to parents into completely foreign territory. All of a sudden, parents no longer had a clear image of the classroom as someplace familiar and predictable. It was flipped, it was personalized or individualized, and heads were down, looking at devices.

The change was relatively swift; the impact, dramatic. Educational institutions had been moving quickly to modernize their infrastructure with a wide array of technology to make administration more efficient and give students the benefits that come with leveraging technology for learning. In turn, parents no longer had a frame of reference to hold on to. It became more difficult for them to imagine what their children were doing at school if not writing essays in notebooks and running through equations on graph paper.

It also all happened before most institutions had a true understanding of what was required to protect student data privacy when sharing the information with technology providers.

We can mark 2013 as the year that parents, parent advocates, and legislators realized that classrooms had changed so much as to be almost wholly unrecognizable. They raised meaningful and important questions about how student personal information was being protected as the technology flooded in; and at the time, many educational institutions, government agencies, and technology providers were not prepared with good answers.

It was clear that the technology already being used in the classroom could have implications for the privacy of student personal information. What was also clear was that many of those implications simply hadn't been considered before the technology had been put in place.

The lack of understanding at the time about how technology operates and how to separate appropriate education technology from that which was not designed to operate in an educational environment helped turn concern from many parent advocates and some legislators into palpable fear.

The climate of fear also was sparked in part by a variety of events that happened in a very short time span.

The questions began with the famous, or now infamous story of inBloom, the technology initiative that promised to increase the possibilities and potential for personalized learning but failed to clearly articulate not only the benefits of the technology, but also how student data would be properly protected.[1] It was a massive, swift, and very public rise and fall, which left the one hundred million dollar project abandoned, closed down before truly getting started.

Around that same time, the country was grappling with the Edward Snowden revelations about government surveillance of personal information, as well as the massive Target data breach, one of the first in the United States to truly resonate with consumers, impacting more than seventy million people and culminating in a financial settlement covering forty-seven states.[2]

Additional scrutiny also was being placed on educational institutions and how they protect the privacy of student personal information when working with technology providers. The *New York Times* published an article by Natasha Singer discussing inBloom, accompanied by a rather eye-catching graphic with the caption, "You for Sale." The article contained a quote that stated unequivocally, "there are too few safeguards for the amount of data collected and transmitted from schools to private companies."[3]

That article sparked Senator Edward Markey (D-MA) to write to then U.S. Department of Education (ED) Secretary Arne Duncan, noting that the *New York Times* article raised questions about how student data might be used by technology companies and "the degree to which student data might be compromised."[4] Senator Markey asked rather pointed questions about whether ED had fully considered the impact of the 2008 and 2011 changes to the Family Educational Rights and Privacy Act (FERPA) on the privacy of student data.

Senator Markey requested a response within three weeks. Almost twelve weeks later, Secretary Duncan responded.[5] Approximately six months later, Senator Markey introduced the "Protecting Student Data Privacy Act of 2014," a federal bill proposing updates to FERPA.

In the meantime, the Fordham Center for Law and Information Policy released a report titled "Privacy and Cloud Computing in Public Schools."[6] The report showcased results of an assessment of how educational institutions managed their legal obligations to protect student data privacy when working with cloud-computing service providers.

It painted a scathing picture of educational institution management over business arrangements with technology providers, detailing a variety of missteps on the part of the institutions related to how they managed their student data privacy obligations when working with technology providers. These included acceptance by educational institutions of contracts in which technology providers gave what amounted to meaningless assurances that they would "not cause the district to fall out of compliance with FERPA."

The report went on to explain that many educational institutions simply didn't seem to understand their data privacy and security responsibilities.[7]

It was a busy year for student data privacy, fraught with revelations and questions but no easy answers. It had a dramatic impact on the awareness among legislators, advocates, parents, educational institutions, and technology providers about the roles, responsibilities, training, and infrastructure required in order to properly protect student data.

Unfortunately, as all of that was unfolding, little attention was paid to educators and how technology use is beneficial in the classroom. The focus was almost solely on what could go wrong with technology providers and student data. A few organizations were speaking up and trying to encourage thoughtful, balanced conversations about the benefits of technology, its utility, risks, and rewards,[8] a movement that continues today.

TEXTBOX 2.1. FERPA AND TECHNOLOGY PROVIDERS

Because FERPA applies to educational institutions and not technology providers, it is incorrect to refer to a technology provider as "FERPA compliant." That would be impossible, or at least, meaningless. A technology provider can ensure that its products may be used in compliance with FERPA and can adhere to the requirements that come with acting in a certain capacity for educational institutions under FERPA, but a technology provider can't fall out of compliance with FERPA because the law doesn't apply to it. It is the educational institution that must comply with FERPA. It's a subtle distinction, and is not meant to suggest that there are not penalties under FERPA that can impact technology providers, or that technology providers don't have responsibilities and requirements to operate in certain ways when working with student data. There are, and they most definitely do. However, the law applies to educational institutions, as we discuss in chapter 5.

However, often those attempts to highlight the need to leverage student data to support students were drowned out by the larger conversation focused on what it meant for student data privacy when the data was in the hands of technology providers and no longer housed within the walls of the educational institution.

As a result of the concern and lingering questions about how educational institutions were managing their privacy responsibilities when sharing data with technology providers, the states sprang into action. Some felt that FERPA didn't provide strong enough protections for student data. Others believed that FERPA contained loopholes that technology providers might exploit in a manner that would put student personal information at risk. Genuine fear of the unknown emerged about how privacy was properly managed with technology provider products being used in schools.

In addition, privacy concerns surfaced in other education discussions, notably in the conversations surrounding a desire to opt out of Common Core standards.[9] In those discussions, concerns over the use of technology providers to facilitate delivery of standardized testing and fears about whether those providers would be able to access student data for noneducational purposes fueled the fire around the education standards.[10]

What followed all of that was a variety of advocacy and legislative activity across the states in what often seemed like frantic attempts to identify and plug real and imagined holes in the existing regulatory framework. Student data privacy bills were drafted at the breakneck pace of well over one hundred bills per year between 2014 and 2016.[11]

The concerns around student data privacy are not going away. They are significant enough to threaten the very real need you have for information to properly educate each of your students and help them find their path to living to their full potential. There is now a near-dizzying array of laws to contend with, and parents continue to question how student data is being protected when it comes to your use of classroom technologies.

From a desire to place limits on classroom screen time to a desire to opt out of certain products, parents have no shortage of concern about what often comes down to your classroom technology management.

This combination of laws and community expectations is a heady mix to wade through and navigate well. Legislators may never finish writing student data privacy laws, and parent advocates may never be satisfied with the protections in place to protect student personal information. In addition, we must contend with the fact that privacy protections are never perfect. Privacy, like security, is a discipline of continuous improvement, never finished but always moving forward.

What can happen, however, is that everyone in the educational institution can accept their part in the responsibility for the proper management, use, and protection of student data, guided by sensible and comprehensive policies and procedures that properly balance data protection requirements with the need to have that student data available to support each student. This often can be enough to provide parents and many legislators with the comfort and confidence that reasonable protections are in place.

This is where you come in. You likely have heard about the importance of protecting student data privacy from your superintendent, principal, chief technology officer, information technology specialist, chief security officer, or, in some cases, simply the person in your school district who handles all things technology. But hearing about it isn't enough. You need to participate actively in the work.

Your educational institution operates under a matrix of laws, regulations, and parent expectations, and you have the power to directly impact your students' privacy for better or for worse. It is an awesome responsibility that you take on simply by handling student data as part of your routine work. In turn, improving your privacy practices also empowers you to ease some of the concerns, fears, and anxieties that your community stakeholders and legislators have over your use of technology in the classroom.

But learning how to ensure that your behavior is not putting your students or the educational institution at risk is not about putting a new set of tasks or responsibilities on your already overflowing plate. The responsibilities always have been there, and you already are making decisions that either positively or negatively impact your students' privacy. This is simply about helping you ensure that those decisions land where you really want them: on the side of making a positive impact on your students.

It can't be emphasized enough that protecting student data privacy is not one person's responsibility. It does not belong to you alone, any more than it belongs solely to the technology team. Everyone in the educational institution has a role to play in protecting the privacy of student data, and doing it well will require some teamwork.

The actions that your educational institution may ask you to take to protect student data privacy may mean a change from how you currently operate. However, it doesn't need to be disruptive. You're already part way there in that perhaps you now understand a bit more about the bigger picture behind all of the scrutiny around student data privacy and that you are already impacting your students' privacy every day. With everyone in your school organization driving toward the same goal—making positive, effective, and efficient use of student data to support the learners in the best way you know how while also protecting their privacy—the task ahead should get even easier.

NOTES AND NEXT STEPS

1. Have you ever had your personal information compromised in a data security incident? Did it change your perception of technology? Do you understand the various ways in which you can manage your personal data privacy?
2. What are some of the ways in which you use technology to facilitate your gathering and use of student data in the classroom and to support creation of individualized learning plans?
3. Do you feel equipped to answer questions from parents about why you use classroom technologies and how you protect the privacy of student data? If not, what information would you need to be better prepared to answer such questions?

Chapter Three

What Information Are
We Trying to Protect?

When we talk about the privacy of student data, we refer to the information we're interested in protecting as personal information or personally identifiable information. Information or types of information that might identify an individual may seem obvious at first glance, but it encompasses a very broad range of sometimes unexpected data elements. Some of the more obvious data points considered to be personal information include a full name, home address, e-mail address, phone number, or a national ID such as a Social Security number. We refer to these as "direct identifiers," and often just one of these data elements identifies an individual.

However, personal information could also be a number of different data elements that alone do not identify anyone but when combined with other data points allow us to know who an individual is.

For example, if someone mentions a student with brown hair, you likely will not know who it is without additional information. "Brown hair" with no other information does not identify an individual. However, if the description is "the boy with brown hair in the third-grade classroom next to yours who had the outburst in the hallway last week," you likely will be able to identify the individual. If that is the case, privacy requirements say that we must treat this information in the same manner as we would if it were the individual's name, e-mail address, or other direct identifier.

Of course, if there had been an outbreak of third-grade boys with brown hair all acting up in the hallway in the same week, you may not be able to discern the specific individual being referenced. The point is: it is not just the data that we need to consider, but the data in context. A combination of indirect identifiers such as hair color, grade level, and other similar factors may combine to identify an individual if the sample size is small enough or if the data elements are unique enough.

The Family Educational Rights and Privacy Act (FERPA), the key federal student data privacy law, is concerned with protecting the privacy of personally identifiable information in the education record. It defines personally identifiable information to include—but not be limited to:[1]

- The student's name;
- The name of the student's parent or other family members;
- The address of the student or the student's family;
- A personal identifier, such as the student's Social Security number, student number, or biometric record;
- Other indirect identifiers, such as the student's date of birth, place of birth, and mother's maiden name;
- Other information that, alone or in combination, is linked or linkable to a specific student that would allow a reasonable person in the school community who does not have personal knowledge of the relevant circumstances to identify the student with reasonable certainty; or
- Information requested by a person who the educational agency or institution reasonably believes knows the identity of the student to whom the education record relates.

Defining "other information that, alone or in combination, is linked or linkable to a specific student that would allow a reasonable person in the school community, who does not have personal knowledge of the relevant circumstances, to identify the student with reasonable certainty" to be personal information can sweep in almost any combination of indirect identifiers and render it to be personal information, depending on the circumstances. As a result, what is and is not personal information can sometimes be fluid, depending on the context and the combination of data factors.

Further complicating matters is that different laws define the personal information that should be protected differently, and some laws don't define it at all.

When it comes to technology use, many laws also consider the identifier of the device to be personal information. Although some might argue that a device ID, an IP address, or other identifier that may persist across the use of the device identifies the machine, not the person, the regulators have rejected that argument.

Most technology providers incorporate a variety of tracking technologies into their products, some of which may gather personal information, such as a

TEXTBOX 3.1.   LEGAL DEFINITIONS OF PROTECTED INFORMATION

In addition to the noted definition of personally identifiable information in FERPA, here are examples of how other privacy laws define the information that must be protected:

Children's Online Privacy Protection Act (COPPA)

COPPA refers to personal information, defined as individually identifiable information collected online from a child under the age of thirteen, including:

- First and last name
- Address or other geolocation information that identifies a street name and city or town
- E-mail address or other online contact information that allows direct contact with a person online, including a screen or user name that functions in that same manner
- Telephone number
- Social Security number
- A persistent identifier that can be used to recognize a user over time and across different websites or online services[1]
- Photograph, video, or audio file that contains a child's image or voice
- Information about the child or the child's parents or legal guardians that the operator collects online from the child and combines with one or more of the above identifiers

State Student Data Privacy Laws

Most state laws intend to protect what they refer to as "covered information," which usually is defined as "personally identifiable information." These laws generally intend to protect personally identifiable student information provided to the technology provider by the student, parent, education institution, or office of education, regardless of what media or format it appears in. However, what constitutes "personally identifiable information" under state student data privacy laws commonly is left undefined.

What is clear is that were it to be defined, the laws would be protecting personal information that is collected by the technology provider through the operation of their product or service, inclusive of information that is "descriptive of a student" or otherwise identifies a student.[2]

(continued)

TEXTBOX 3.1. *(continued)*

Notes

1. "Children's Online Privacy Protection Act." https://www.ecfr.gov/cgi-bin/text
-idx?SID=4939e77c77a1a1a08c1cbf905fc4b409&node=16%3A1.0.1.3.36&rgn=div5.
Although the persistent identifier that can be used to recognize a user over time and
across unrelated websites or online services is personal information under COPPA,
operators subject to COPPA are not required to obtain prior consent to collect the
persistent identifier and use it for specific functions deemed support for the internal
operations. These are activities necessary to:

(a) maintain or analyze the functioning of the website or online service;
(b) perform network communications;
(c) authenticate users of, or personalize the content on, the website or online service;
(d) serve contextual advertising on the website or online service or cap the frequency
    of advertising;
(e) protect the security or integrity of the user, website, or online service;
(f) ensure legal or regulatory compliance; or
(g) fulfill a request of a child as permitted by §§ 312.5(c)(3) and (4); so long as the infor-
    mation collected for the activities listed in paragraphs (a)–(g) is not used or disclosed
    to contact a specific individual, including through behavioral advertising, to amass
    a profile on a specific individual, or for any other purpose.

2. "Student Online Personal Information Protection Act," https://leginfo.legislature
.ca.gov/faces/billNavClient.xhtml?bill_id=201320140SB1177.

persistent identifier, in a manner that is rather passive to the user. Sometimes tracking is necessary in order for the technology to function.

For example, technology providers need to have a way to recognize you when you are logged in. They may need to remember the last bit of progress you made in a program so that you don't have to start from the beginning every time you log back in, but instead can pick up where you left off. That's all done via technology that tracks and stores some data related to your use of the product and the device.

Other use cases for tracking technologies include helping to serve content or advertising. Tracking technologies also permit technology providers to gather information useful to assess the product performance, troubleshoot issues, and improve the product. This might include information about the number of product users, how much time users spend in the product, what areas of the product are used most often, in what order users navigate to different features in the product, and what areas of the product are not performing as expected.

In still other cases, the technology might be tracking keystrokes, how long it takes a student to answer a question, how many right and wrong answers a student recorded, what types of questions were answered correctly and what types incorrectly, and how rigorous the questions could be before the student was unable to proceed further.

Some of this tracking is there simply to make sure the product works for you, some of it is to gather information for the technology provider for internal purposes, and some of it is to serve the learning purpose. Of course, some of it might serve multiple purposes.

Sorting that out is part of the challenge of identifying what information is considered to be personal information requiring protection, what practices are legitimate and lawful in a school setting, and what information and use practices might compromise the privacy of your students or simply not be legal when the information being gathered is student data.

When it comes to student data privacy, we're concerned with protecting student personal information, which can take on many of the forms described above. It may be a direct identifier that you easily recognize as personal, or it may be a combination of indirect identifiers. You may be readily aware that you or your students are providing personal information because a colleague or a technology provider asks you for it, or you may be aware only after reading the privacy policy, because the technology provider collects it without assistance when your students use a product you bring into the classroom.

Regardless of how it is collected or the form it takes, all such personal information is subject to protection under student data privacy laws.

NOTES AND NEXT STEPS

1. Consider all of the ways you interact with student personal information every day. Taking attendance, grading exams, making a video recording of your students or recording their voices all include you managing their personal information. Would you think differently about how you protect that information if it were your bank information or national ID? How might your students or parents react if the information you manage were shared outside your classroom with someone not authorized to have that access?
2. What do you think your students would consider to be personal information worthy of protecting? How does that compare to the legal definitions of personal information?
3. Begin to assess the ways in which the technology products you bring into the classroom might be collecting your students' personal information. How much do you know about their data privacy practices? What of those data privacy practices have you communicated to parents?

Chapter Four

Key Privacy Concepts

It's impossible to talk about student data privacy without discussing the legal requirements around it. This book is not intended to be a legal guide, and it assumes that you do not need to or even perhaps desire to become an expert in the laws. However, student data privacy laws are a critical part of the foundation on which we must make decisions about handling student personal information and bringing technology into the classroom.

The idea here is not to require that you understand every nuance, every nook and cranny in each law. The point is simply to provide you with a solid framework through which you can build your fluency in the basic requirements around effective protection of student data.

That lens will help you better understand why your educational institution policies are in place, make better privacy decisions for your students, make more informed decisions about what technology products and services to use in the classroom, and know when to bring a privacy decision to the attention of your leadership or technology team. It also will empower you to have more constructive conversations with your institution leadership and technology teams about how to collaborate on data protection without stifling the work you do in the classroom or the manner in which you operate.

Given the complexity of the legal requirements surrounding student data privacy, it helps to begin by breaking down the laws into their primary concepts. For that, when it comes to privacy laws, we turn to the Fair Information Practice Principles (FIPPS).[1] Whether by design or by accident, almost every privacy law draws from the FIPPS. These principles were written in the 1970s, and they provide some basic considerations for positive privacy practices. The FIPPS will appear in a slightly different format, depending on which source you use. However, the ideas behind them are nearly universal, and they are fairly easy to understand.

Here are the FIPPS and some examples of how you might see them in action:

Table 4.1.   Fair Information Practice Principles in Action

Fair Information Practice Principles:	*Concepts in Action:*
Transparency: provide clear notice to individuals about what personal information is collected, used, shared, and maintained.	Before collecting, using, or sharing personal information about someone, we need to tell them what personal information we intend to collect, what we plan to do with it, and with whom we might share it. The most common example of this type of transparency is the privacy policy on your educational institution website or on every piece of technology you use that collects personal information from or about you or your students.
Individual Participation: ensure that individuals are able to review, copy, and correct or amend their personal information; information should be collected with consent or knowledge of the individual.	Before collecting personal information from someone, we must first request and receive that person's permission. In the case of a student under the age of eighteen, or who has not yet matriculated at a higher education institution, that permission is managed by the parent or legal guardian. In addition, the individual should be able to review their personal information, keep it accurate, and keep a copy of it.
Purpose Specification: articulate the authority that permits collection of personal information and the purposes for which it is intended to be used.	There should always be a specific reason and intended use for each item of personal information we collect, and we should clearly articulate why we are authorized to collect it. Sometimes the authorization comes in the form of permission that a parent or adult student has provided to your educational institution. In other cases, the technology provider that manages an app or website you use in the classroom might be authorized as a result of the contract you have agreed to with them by clicking to agree to their Terms of Use. We'll review authorization examples and requirements in chapter 5.

Fair Information Practice Principles:	Concepts in Action:
Data Minimization: only collect personal information that is directly relevant and necessary for the specified purpose, use and disclose it only as necessary to fulfill the purpose for which it was collected, and retain it only for as long as is necessary to fulfill that purpose.	We should never collect or access personal information just for the sake of having the data. Think about your own online habits. If you shop online, you wouldn't expect everyone at the store to have access to your information. It would be an invasion of your privacy if they did. Instead, you might expect only those individuals who need to look at your data to fulfill your order or keep the system running to have access. Even then, we would expect those individuals only to need access to a limited amount of information to do their job. The person fulfilling the order would need to know what you ordered to package it properly, but if that person is not responsible for processing payment, they shouldn't have access to your billing information.

The same holds true for student data. If we collect more information than we need, or if we access data when we have no need to, it is an invasion of privacy.

Remember that although data is an asset, it's also a liability. Whatever data we collect, we have to protect, and data protection often is a complex and expensive proposition. That's also why we delete data once we no longer need it. Personal information left in place when it's not needed is simply a risk. |
| Use Limitation: use personal information only for the specified purpose for which it was collected. | If we give our personal information to a company to make a purchase, we expect it to use that information only to fulfill that purpose, unless we agreed to allow its use for something else— perhaps to subscribe to a mailing list—at the time that we provided the information. However, we should never be surprised at what our personal information is being used for because we should always have given permission for that use. Similarly, personal information may only be used for the purpose for which it was provided, and the companies that operate your classroom technologies must do the same. |

(continued)

Table 4.1. *(continued)*

Fair Information Practice Principles:	*Concepts in Action:*
Data Quality and Integrity: ensure that personal information remains accurate, timely, relevant, and complete.	Inaccurate or out-of-date data is not useful, and it can be harmful. Imagine that you once had a poor credit score. If you took steps to improve it over the years, but all of your creditors still were using the outdated information, that could be harmful to you and could limit your opportunities. The same holds true for your students. The information the educational institution holds about them needs to remain up to date and accurate. This helps ensure that we are able to leverage the right data in the right ways to support students, and helps us to avoid causing harm with inaccuracies and data that is no longer relevant.
Security: protect personal information through appropriately reasonable security standards against risks such as loss, unauthorized access or use, destruction, modification, or unintended or inappropriate disclosure.	Data security is critical to protecting personal information from unauthorized access. Personal information should not be collected if it cannot be properly protected. Not all personal information is equally sensitive, so not all data needs to be protected with the same measures. For example, a student's name is not as sensitive as a Social Security number or a name combined with health information. However, protecting personal information is of paramount importance. Our behaviors can help keep the information secure or open it up to access by those looking to do harm. The responsibility then, is to adhere to your institution's strong security requirements to keep the data from prying eyes.
Accountability and Auditing: be accountable for complying with these principles, provide training to all individuals who use the personal information, and audit the use of personal information to demonstrate compliance with the relevant privacy protection requirements.	Policies and processes for handling personal information are necessary, but if we're not monitoring how everyone across an organization is complying with those policies and processes, we won't know where things aren't working well and where we may still have risk. Of course, knowing how to comply is made easier if we understand why all of these requirements are in place, which is where training comes in. The more we know about how to best protect student data, the better we are at it.

NOTES AND NEXT STEPS

1. Consider the FIPPS in relation to how your educational institution asks you to protect student personal information. Are you able to see any of them start to come to life in the fabric of your educational institution's data governance policies?
2. Might certain FIPPS concepts inform your classroom discussions about data privacy? Might you put any into practice in a way that your students could model?
3. Do the FIPPS concepts align with questions you hear from parents in your community about how student data privacy is protected? Where do the questions differ?

Chapter Five

Family Educational Rights and Privacy Act

In the United States, the current regulatory frameworks place special protections on data in accordance with the sensitivity of that data. As such, privacy of student data is heavily regulated. Other heavily regulated data includes financial data, health data, and personal information collected online from young children.

This differs somewhat from how data protection is handled in the EU and in many regions around the globe. In those regions, data is not protected by sector, but instead the regulations protect all personal information. Even so, special protections are provided to certain sensitive data, including data that reveals racial or ethnic origin, political opinions, religious or philosophical beliefs, or trade union membership, genetic data, biometric data, or data concerning a person's sex life or sexual orientation.

For our purposes, let's look at the key U.S. federal student data privacy law that you are working in and around every day in the classroom.

FAMILY EDUCATIONAL RIGHTS AND PRIVACY ACT (FERPA)[1]

FERPA probably could best be referred to as the grandfather of student data privacy laws. Passed in 1974, but updated via guidance issued in 2008 and 2011, FERPA is enforced by the U.S. Department of Education (ED) and applies to educational institutions that receive ED funding. Even if your institution is not receiving ED funding, understanding FERPA will help you build a strong foundation for protecting student data privacy and work in compliance with your state student data privacy laws, most of which draw some of their fundamental requirements from FERPA.

At a high level, FERPA accomplishes two objectives:

1. It establishes rights for parents (inclusive of legal guardians) and students who have reached the age of eighteen or who have matriculated at a higher education institution ("eligible students") around the information in the student's education record, and
2. It establishes the conditions under which personal information from a student's education record may be disclosed.

To be more specific, FERPA establishes rights for parents and eligible students to do any of the following:

- Review and inspect the student's education record;
- Request that the educational institution amend or correct information in the student's education record that the parent or eligible student believes to be inaccurate, misleading, or otherwise in violation of the student's privacy rights;
- Have a hearing in the event that a request to amend or correct information in the student's record is denied.

Requests to inspect the education record must be fulfilled within forty-five days (sooner under some state student data privacy law requirements). In addition, because compiling the education record in response to such requests may be complex, your educational institution likely has provided you with policies and procedures for referring requests from parents and eligible students to access the education record or exercise their other rights under FERPA to a central administrative office.

Each year, your educational institution must notify parents and eligible students of their rights under FERPA and how they may go about exercising those rights. This notice must be "effectively provided" for the disabled and, in the case of elementary and secondary institutions, to parents whose primary home language is not English.

Importantly, FERPA does not allow personally identifiable information in the student's education record to be disclosed without prior signed and dated written consent of the parent or eligible student, except in certain limited circumstances. Those circumstances include disclosure to a number of entities, including:

- Another school to which a student is transferring;
- Certain officials for audit or evaluation purposes;
- Appropriate parties in connection with determining eligibility in response to a financial aid application;

TEXTBOX 5.1.   UNDERSTANDING THE EDUCATION RECORD

Just what is the education record? At its simplest, it is just about any and every bit of information directly related to a student and maintained by the educational institution or a third party acting for the institution. However, there are some exceptions:

The term education record does not include:

1. Records that are kept in the sole possession of the maker, are used only as a personal memory aid, and are not accessible or revealed to any other person except a temporary substitute for the maker of the record.
2. Records of the law enforcement unit of an educational agency or institution, subject to the provisions of §99.8 of FERPA.[1]
3. (i) Records relating to an individual who is employed by an educational agency or institution, that:
   A. Are made and maintained in the normal course of business;
   B. Relate exclusively to the individual in that individual's capacity as an employee; and
   C. Are not available for use for any other purpose.
   (ii) Records relating to an individual in attendance at the agency or institution who is employed as a result of his or her status as a student are education records.
4. Records on a student who is eighteen years of age or older, or is attending an institution of postsecondary education, that are:
   (i) Made or maintained by a physician, psychiatrist, psychologist, or other recognized professional or paraprofessional acting in his or her professional capacity or assisting in a paraprofessional capacity;
   (ii) Made, maintained, or used only in connection with treatment of the student; and
   (iii) Disclosed only to individuals providing the treatment, provided, however, that "treatment" does not include remedial educational activities or activities that are part of the program of instruction at the agency or institution; and
5. Records created or received by an educational agency or institution after an individual is no longer a student in attendance and that are not directly related to the individual's attendance as a student.
6. Grades on peer-graded papers before they are collected and recorded by a teacher.

Note

1. "Family Educational Rights and Privacy Act," 20 U.S.C. § 1232g; 34 CFR Part 99 §99.8.

- Organizations conducting certain studies for or on behalf of the educational institution to develop, validate, or administer predictive tests or student aid programs, or to improve instruction;
- Accrediting organizations;
- Authorized parties in a court case when necessary to comply with a judicial order or lawful subpoena;
- Appropriate officials in the case of health and safety emergencies;
- State and local authorities within a juvenile justice system, in accordance with state law.

Some of these use cases also are restricted by additional conditions that must be met prior to releasing the personally identifiable information. Your educational institution likely has policies in place to ensure that personally identifiable student information is not shared for any of the purposes noted above except in accordance with careful procedures to ensure that the use case meets the requirements laid out in FERPA.

Personally identifiable student information from the education records may be shared without prior written consent of the parent or eligible student in two circumstances that are directly relevant to classroom practices: sharing directory information and sharing personally identifiable student information with school officials.

Directory Information

Educational institutions may designate certain information about students to be directory information. Under FERPA, directory information is information that is not considered to be harmful or an invasion of privacy if released. It may include a student's name, address, telephone number, e-mail address, photo, date and place of birth, major field of study, grade level, enrollment status, dates of attendance, participation in officially recognized activities and sports, weight and height of members of athletic teams, degrees, honors and awards, and the most recent educational agency or institution attended.

Directory information may not include a student's Social Security number. It may include a student ID or other unique personal identifier used to access or communicate in electronic systems or displayed on a student ID, only when that identifier cannot be used to access education records except in connection with another authentication factor, such as a password or PIN.

Each year, the educational institution must provide parents and eligible students with a notice that includes the types of personally identifiable information that it has designated as directory information, provide the individual with the opportunity to opt out of having some or all of those types of information designated as directory information (and thus shared without their prior written consent), and the deadline for notifying the educational institution of the desire to opt out.

Note that this exception for sharing directory information without prior written consent is not intended to be used when sharing personally identifiable student information with educational institution partners or technology providers, including any of the companies operating apps and websites used in the classroom. It is simply intended to allow educational institutions to go about their routine operations and to engage in traditional school activities, such as publishing a yearbook and disclosing the list of students on the school sports teams or in a program for a school play, without having to obtain prior written consent for those activities.

In addition, your institution may have created a "limited-release" directory information policy. This is a "privacy forward" policy in which the institution defines not only what personally identifiable information it will categorize as directory information, but also the circumstances under which it will disclose that information. For example, an institution may choose to designate student photos as directory information, but only for the purpose of publication in the yearbook. It's important to stay current on your institution's directory information policies, which may change over time.

School Officials

When sharing personally identifiable student information from education records with technology providers, it's more appropriate to designate the technology operator as a school official if the technology provider qualifies as such. School officials are employees (including you), consultants, vendors, volunteers, and other parties who have a legitimate educational interest in receiving personally identifiable student information from education records. Under FERPA, as a school official you are permitted to access personally identifiable student information without prior written consent from the parent or eligible student only when the following conditions are met:

1. You have a legitimate educational interest in the personal information in the education record; and
2. The educational institution uses "reasonable methods" to ensure that you obtain access to only those education records in which you have a legitimate educational interest. These reasonable methods may be physical or technological controls, or a policy that effectively limits access to only the personally identifiable student information in the education record in which you have a legitimate educational interest.[2]

Your educational institution must inform parents and eligible students each year about how it considers and qualifies parties to be school officials with a legitimate educational interest in the personal information from the education record.

As an educator, you have an obvious legitimate educational interest in accessing certain personally identifiable student data, and FERPA establishes that you may do so without getting written consent from the parent or eligible student in advance. However, it is the legitimate educational interest that informs the boundaries of your authority to access personally identifiable student information.

FERPA does not specifically define the legitimate educational interest. However, it does make clear that access to the personally identifiable information in the student education records must be limited to "need to know." That is, the regulation requires that you have access to only the personally identifiable student information that is deemed necessary for you to perform your job.

Your school or district should have a policy that defines the legitimate educational interest. This policy should have been shared with you and with parents. That is what governs the purpose for which you may have access to student data and may illustrate general limitations on that access.

Those limitations may be further defined in additional educational institution policies for security and related data protection purposes. As noted by the Institute of Education Sciences National Center for Education Statistics, in many cases that legitimate educational interest is something that will need to be determined by the educational institution based on the circumstances and context.

They suggest some examples that may or may not be part of your institution's policy statement, such as substantiation demonstrating that the information being accessed is:

- Necessary to perform a job as documented in the job description or contract;
- To be used only for official school purposes;
- Relevant to accomplishing a school function or making a determination about the student;
- To be used in a manner consistent with why it is maintained.[3]

To comply with the regulation, at a high level, many educational institution technology teams quite reasonably may deny access to personally identifiable information related to students who are not in your classroom. They also may deny access to personally identifiable information related to students who are in your classroom but that educational institution leaders have determined is not necessary for performance of your role.

Although that may create a healthy tension among leadership, the technology team, and teachers, the access limitations are in place to protect student data privacy in the ways mandated by the laws.

Restricting access to data is one of the most common and fundamental security protections, short of not collecting the data at all. It often is referred to as "rule/role-based access," meaning that who has access to what data depends in part on whether the data access is necessary in order to do the job. Simply stated, the more people who have access to certain data, the greater the privacy and security risks, so rule/role-based access is foundational to any data protection program.

Clearly you need a wide array of student information in order to perform your job well, and the data protection regulations and norms do not intend to suggest otherwise. However, a variety of real-world examples show educators having access to more personally identifiable student information than is truly necessary for the job at hand, which creates unnecessary risk. The right balance needs to be struck between ensuring that you have everything you need to truly inform instruction for each of your students and overloading you with information you don't need or use that puts the educational institution at risk.

Striking the right balance requires careful consideration for your work, the regulations, district policies, and community expectations. Hopefully, you now have more information to help facilitate a collaborative discussion about access in your organization if you have reason to believe that current policies are too restrictive. You may also want to initiate discussion if you believe your current access to personally identifiable student information is too permissive.

In most cases, access to personally identifiable student information is restricted to protect you, your students, and the institution. Either way, the law demands a documented, legitimate educational interest in order for access to be provided.

Once you have access to personally identifiable student information to support the legitimate educational interest, you are not permitted under the regulation to do anything more with it except to meet that interest. You are not permitted to share it with anyone unless authorized; and, in that case, in the absence of prior written consent from the parent or eligible student, or some other exception to the consent requirement in FERPA, it may only be shared with someone who has also been designated as a school official with a legitimate educational interest in that data.

Essentially, the law sets out a right to access the education record as a privilege, and every employee with access to the data has a role to play in supporting that legal compliance in keeping with the educational institution's policies. Check with your institution policy before sharing personally identifiable student information with anyone, even other teachers.

We're only human, and sometimes our best instincts drive us to run afoul of this part of the regulation. School employees sometimes ask for access to more personally identifiable student information than they truly need. Educational institutions don't always have the proper measures in place to ensure that you aren't given more than what you want. When parents call to talk about how their child is doing in a particular class, a well-meaning teacher also may look up information about the child's sibling in another class.

The law tells us we need to avoid falling into those traps. You have enough responsibility on your plate: don't take on responsibility for accessing or sharing student data when it is not yours to begin with.

An outside party, such as a technology provider, might qualify as a school official in your educational institution. If it does, sharing of certain personally identifiable student information, with the proper protections in place, might be appropriate. Consult with your educational institution's policy on what entities may be qualified as school officials when considering the technology products you would like to bring into the classroom.

Part of assessing a technology provider's qualifications to be a school official is to establish that it performs a function for which your institution would otherwise use its employees. Under the law, if the company is not performing such a function, it can't qualify as a school official, and so personally identifiable student data may not be shared with that company without prior written consent from the parents or eligible students.

Once it is established that a party has a legitimate educational interest in receiving personally identifiable student data and would be performing a function for which the institution might otherwise use school employees, the party may—if the educational institution chooses to do so—be designated as a school official.

Note that the technology provider doesn't make this determination. The educational institution does. If you are bringing apps and websites into the classroom without vetting them first through a centralized process at your institution or working with your leadership or technology team, appreciate that you are making a variety of legal and policy determinations, including whether to qualify each technology provider as a school official.

When it comes to sharing personally identifiable student information with a school official, the educational institution must maintain "direct control" over the school official's use and maintenance of the education records. When it comes to technology providers, this direct control most often is expressed in a contractual agreement between the institution and the school official.

Elements of direct control expressed in contracts might include provisions documenting what personally identifiable information will be disclosed, the educational purpose for which the information may be used, how long and under what conditions it may be maintained, when it must be deleted, if it must be returned before being deleted, and how the institution may access, amend, and correct the personally identifiable information for its own purposes or in response to a valid request from a parent or eligible student exercising their rights under FERPA.

TEXTBOX 5.2. ESTABLISHING "DIRECT CONTROL"

Direct control means that the educational institution chooses what happens with the education records.

An educational institution establishing direct control over how a technology provider uses and maintains the data is similar to how a company manages employee conduct: policies, procedures, and in some cases, contracts set expectations for behavior; and people (or, in the case of technology providers, entities) are held accountable for compliance.

Expectations for behavior for a technology provider might include:

- Confirmation that the personally identifiable information from education records:
  - May only be used to serve the educational institution purpose;
  - May not be used or disclosed for any other purpose without prior written consent of the parent or eligible student;
  - Remains under the direct control of the institution.
- Details of the physical, technical, and administrative security controls that must be in place to protect the personal information;
- How data will be made available in response to a parent or eligible student request to review their education record;
- When personally identifiable information will be deleted and/or returned;
- That any changes to the terms require mutual consent.

Control usually is established with a contract. Whether it's a click-wrap agreement or a signed document, the contract establishes legally binding requirements for behavior. It should include provisions that specify what the educational institution requires of the technology provider, particularly in terms of what personally identifiable student information may be collected, how it may be used and handled, and how it may be shared; and what happens to the data when the contract ends, all in the manner that the technology provider can and does implement.

Educational institutions also must ensure that as school officials, technology providers are given access only to the personally identifiable information in the education records in which they have a legitimate educational interest. This is just one of the reasons why it's important to understand exactly what elements of the education record, including the personally identifiable information, will be collected and created by the technology providers whose products you decide to bring into the classroom.

The technology provider must then only use the personally identifiable student information from the education records to serve the legitimate educational purpose, and the educational institution must maintain direct control over that information. If the technology provider would like to use the information for any other purpose, it must first obtain prior written consent from the parent or eligible student. State laws and your educational institution may put additional restrictions on what the data may be used for, with or without the written consent.

De-identified Data

An educational institution may disclose student information without prior consent from the parent or eligible student if the information has been properly de-identified before being shared.

De-identification is a complex undertaking that requires removal, obfuscation, and masking of certain data fields, including the obvious identifiable information and careful consideration for whether the remaining data may reasonably identify an individual.

According to ED, de-identification is considered successful "when there is no reasonable basis to believe that the remaining information in the records can be used to identify an individual."[4] This "reasonable determination" may be made only when consideration is also given to information that already may be publicly or readily available, what data may be released on other occasions, and whether the sample size is large enough to ensure that individuals are not identifiable to those who might know them.

It requires, for example, removal of not just the obvious direct identifiers, such as names and student e-mail addresses, but also consideration for which of the indirect identifiers might need to be removed or altered, such as grades or class schedules, when the sample size or context might cause that information to render an individual identifiable to someone in the local community.

Think of it this way: as discussed in chapter 3, you don't necessarily need to know the name of a student in order to identify the individual. You may be able to identify a student based on age, physical description, class schedule, and behavior. However, if we have a large number of students who meet those same characteristics, you may not be able to identify a particular individual. Consideration for these types of scenarios, as well as the data that may have been or could be released as directory information, is part of the standard that FERPA requires when creating de-identified data that can be released without prior parent or eligible student consent.

When dealing with technology-enabled data collection, biometric data, keystroke data, or other personal elements also need to be taken into consideration, as do device identifiers and browsing behaviors. It's imperative to read and understand the privacy policy to know what personally identifiable information is being collected. As such, it can take time to determine whether the data a particular technology provider is receiving is personally identifiable information, subject to protection under the law.

It's yet another reason to act thoughtfully and methodically to consider student data privacy requirements before bringing technology into the classroom.

Collaborate with your technology team to increase your understanding of these data privacy considerations. The more you understand the sometimes fine distinctions between what data may be used when, where, and by whom, with and without prior written parent or eligible student consent, the better you will be able to partner with your technology team on a sensible way to assess the privacy practices of classroom technologies.

Record-Keeping Requirements

FERPA contains a variety of record-keeping requirements with which your educational institution must comply. It requires that educational institutions keep a record of each request for access to and disclosure of personally identifiable information from the education records of each student. Your institution must keep a record not just of every individual who requests access to personally identifiable information from the education records, but also of every technology provider that might collect personally identifiable information from or about your students.

The records must note which parties have requested or received the personally identifiable information from the education records, and for what legitimate purpose. These records must be kept for as long as the institution maintains the student's education record, a period of time often dictated by the state student data retention laws.

As the gatekeeper for your students, then, it's critically important to keep track of all of the apps, websites, and other technologies you bring into the classroom and to understand what personally identifiable information they receive. That becomes part of the record your educational institution must maintain in compliance with FERPA.

Records also must be kept on state and local educational authorities and federal agencies and officials that are permitted to disclose personally identifiable information from education records without having obtained prior parent or eligible student consent.

Enforcement

FERPA is enforced by the Family Policy Compliance Office (FPCO) of ED. The office is authorized to review complaints it receives alleging noncompliance with FERPA and investigate those complaints as it sees fit. When an educational institution is found to be operating in violation of FERPA, ED generally will issue notice explaining the specific steps that are both necessary and expected in order to comply with the law. It also will establish a time frame within which those steps must be completed.

FERPA is part of the General Education Provisions Act,[5] which requires that educational institutions meet certain obligations when they receive federal education funds. If an institution does not comply with an enforcement notice, ED may compel compliance by issuing a cease and desist order, withholding funding it previously had provided until compliance is achieved, or terminating an educational institution's eligibility to receive such funding.

In addition, if ED finds that a third party, such as a technology provider, that had received access to personally identifiable student information from education records has redisclosed any of that information without obtaining the necessary prior parent or eligible student consents, or otherwise caused the educational institution to fall out of compliance with FERPA, ED may require that the institution not allow the third party access to personally identifiable information from its education records for at least five years.

NOTES AND NEXT STEPS

1. Review your educational institution's definitions of legitimate educational interests and how your institution qualifies parties to be school officials. Is there information that surprises you, seems outdated, or requires explanation? Consult with your technology team or institution leadership to ensure that you understand how to implement the institution's policies related to FERPA compliance.
2. Assess the student personal information that is available to you. Does it seem appropriate and limited to what is necessary for you to perform well in your role? Do you have permission to access any student personal information that you don't use? Do you have access to student data from

students who are not in your classroom? Why or why not? What is the legitimate educational interest, as articulated by your educational institution, that such access serves?

3. Are you familiar with the ways in which your educational institution is transparent with parents and eligible students about how student personal information is collected, used, and shared? Have you seen the privacy notices that your institution sends home every year? Do they properly reflect how you operate with technology in the classroom?

Chapter Six

Still More Laws

FERPA is the backbone of U.S. student data privacy law, but other regulations are also critical.

As you did when reading about FERPA, keep the FIPPS in mind as you read and consider how the laws draw on those concepts.

PROTECTION OF PUPIL RIGHTS AMENDMENT (PPRA)

The Protection of Pupil Rights Amendment[1] provides important guidance and requirements about the collection of sensitive information in the classroom, as well as limitations on use of personally identifiable student data for marketing purposes.

PPRA applies to state educational agencies, local educational agencies, or others who receive funding from ED. The penalties for noncompliance with PPRA are quite similar to those in FERPA: investigation and notice of required remedies are enforced in large part by the ability of ED to withhold federal funding or terminate an educational institution's eligibility to receive federal funding in order to compel compliance.

Unlike FERPA, which applies rather broadly to the student education record and is particularly concerned with disclosure of personally identifiable information from the education record, PPRA is focused on information collected directly from students via surveys, analyses, or evaluation about these sensitive topics:

- Political affiliations or beliefs of the student or the student's parents;
- Mental or psychological problems of the student or the student's family;

- Sexual behaviors or attitudes;
- Illegal, antisocial, self-incriminating, or demeaning behavior;
- Critical appraisals of other individuals with whom the student has close family relationships;
- Legally recognized privileged or analogous relationships, such as those of lawyers, physicians, and ministers;
- Religious practices, affiliations, or beliefs of the student or the student's parent;
- Income (other than what legally is permissible to determine eligibility for participation in a program or for receiving financial assistance).

PPRA requires that, in the event that a survey, analysis, evaluation, or similar measure will be asking students about these sensitive topics, the educational institution must provide advance notice to parents and obtain their prior consent when that survey is funded in whole or in part by ED. In this sense, while FERPA requires the educational institution to provide parents and eligible students with access to the student's education record, PPRA requires that the educational institution ask permission before collecting certain information in the first place.

When a survey involving a sensitive topic is not funded by ED, the educational institution still, at a minimum, must provide annual notice to parents at the beginning of the school year about its intent to conduct those surveys. The notice must explain the anticipated dates of any such surveys and allow parents to opt their child out of participating. The institution must also advise parents of their right to review your instructional materials used in connection with such a survey and as part of the curriculum.

Do you ever conduct surveys or analyses that touch on any of these sensitive subjects in your classroom, or do you work with technology providers that facilitate such activities for you? Do you have guidance from your educational institution's leadership about the boundaries for those materials? Do you know when to alert leadership that you'll be conducting a survey involving a sensitive topic so that the necessary parent notices and consents may be managed?

Even if you are not asking students to respond to survey questions about a sensitive topic or are not conducting what the regulation refers to as an analysis or evaluation, do you ever discuss any of these sensitive topics in the classroom? If so, be sure you are handling that in compliance with your educational institution's policy and PPRA.

If you are unsure of that policy, or if one doesn't exist, have a conversation with your educational institution's leadership. Be sure you have what you need to ensure that you're properly protecting student privacy and doing your part to maintain your institution's compliance with PPRA.

Similar notice must be provided to parents in advance of any nonemergency, invasive physical exam or screening when it is required as a condition of attendance, administered by the school, and not necessary to protect the immediate health and safety of any student.

PPRA also is concerned with policy development governing this work. In the event that an educational institution has not yet established policies for managing the notice and consent process, as well as the process for granting access to the surveys and related instructional materials to parents who request to review the information, the educational institution must work with parents in the community to develop policies that encompass:

- The right of parents to inspect a survey created by the educational institution or a third party before the survey is administered or distributed to students, and the process for responding to such requests from parents;
- How the educational institution will protect the privacy of students when the survey contains any of the sensitive topics described above;
- The right of parents to inspect instructional material that is part of the educational curriculum, and how the institution will grant such requests for access;
- Administration of physical exams or screenings of students;
- The rights of parents to opt out of use and disclosure of their child's information for certain commercial purposes;
- The right of parents to inspect any instrument used to collect personal information from students for marketing or sales purposes before the instrument is implemented, and how the educational institution will provide such access.

As an educator, your voice is important in the conversation as well, so if these policies have not yet been established, build the connection with educational institution leaders so that you may be included in the discussions.

Note that, unlike FERPA, which permits use of personally identifiable student information only to serve the legitimate educational interest, PPRA does permit use of personally identifiable student information for limited marketing purposes. Even then, those marketing purposes are related to education: what is permitted under PPRA is use of personally identifiable student information for marketing of educational materials and postsecondary pathways.

PPRA allows an educational institution to collect, use, or disclose personally identifiable student information without adhering to the policy-writing requirements when the information is used to develop, evaluate, or provide educational products or services, such as:

- College or other postsecondary education or military recruitment;
- Book clubs, magazines, and programs providing access to low-cost literary products;
- Curriculum and instructional materials used by elementary and secondary schools;
- Tests and assessments used by elementary and secondary schools to provide cognitive, evaluative, diagnostic, clinical, aptitude, or achievement information about students, as well as analysis and release of aggregated results;
- Fund-raising for school- or education-related activities in the form of student sale of products or services;
- Student recognition programs.

However, the mere fact that a law permits certain activities does not mean that an educational institution must engage in those activities, and your institution may not. Each educational institution must determine what it deems acceptable, and many state laws have, in effect, closed the marketing allowance in PPRA by restricting use of any student data for targeted marketing purposes.

As such, the determination of whether your educational institution will permit such practices involves leadership assessment of a variety of factors, including not only legal allowances, but also the values, norms, and expectations of the community in which the institution operates, the data protection capabilities of the institution, the repercussions for restricting or permitting certain legally permissible activities, and the institution's general mission and vision related to collection and use of personally identifiable student information.

Be sure that you are familiar with and understand your educational institution's policies around asking students questions about the sensitive topics covered by PPRA and any limitations it has set on use of student data for educational and commercial purposes. Remember that the limitations apply to both your own materials and to any technology products and services you bring into the classroom.

STATE STUDENT DATA PRIVACY LAWS

In the U.S. K–12 ecosystem, it's difficult to overstate the impact that state student data privacy laws are having on the ways in which student personal information must be protected. Beginning in 2014, as a result of the then unprecedented attention to privacy protections for student data and how educational institutions were managing their responsibilities and relationships with technology providers, almost every state proposed or passed its own law, and sometimes multiple laws, directly regulating student data privacy.[2]

Many of these laws are enforced against technology providers and not educational institutions, although some exceptions apply.[3]

It would be impossible to catalog all of the state laws here. However, do review your state student data privacy laws so that you can better understand and comply with your educational institution's student data privacy policies and procedures.

A few common concepts emerge across most of the state student data privacy laws that we can explore.

To begin with, state student data privacy laws are applicable broadly. Unlike FERPA and PPRA, they are not limited to only those educational institutions that receive government funding. So, even if your institution does not need to adhere to FERPA and PPRA, your state student data privacy laws may apply. In general, the laws tend to focus on protecting the privacy, security, and integrity of student personal information in alignment with four key concepts, which you will recognize from our discussion of FIPPS:

1. Control
2. Access
3. Use restrictions
4. Transparency

Control

Many state student data privacy laws reiterate the existing FERPA requirement that an educational institution maintain "direct control" over the education record when working with technology providers. That control is meant to ensure that when student personal information is collected by or shared with a technology provider, it is used only to serve the school purpose.

In addition, some of the laws specifically mandate that the educational institution's control and the limitations in place regarding what the data may be used for extend to not only the technology providers, but also to third-party organizations that may partner with technology providers.

It is quite common for technology providers to rely on external partners to provide services and support for certain product functions. Examples of services that may be outsourced include cloud storage, data analytics, video players, and customer support. In many cases, state laws require that the data privacy and security practices of the technology provider, and the limitations imposed by its agreement with the educational institution, extend to any of its service providers that may need to receive student personal information in order for the technology to operate as expected.

Certain states, notably California, Colorado, Connecticut, Louisiana, and New York, require specific contractual provisions or minimum thresholds for subject matter that must be addressed in agreements between educational institutions and technology providers.

One important impact for you to consider, then, is if, when bringing technology into the classroom through a click-wrap agreement (generally terms of use that appear online with a button that you click to accept those terms, indicating your agreement) and without aid of a larger vetting process, the terms you agree to comply with your state's legal requirements for a contract with an education technology provider.

A variety of provisions in state laws also require technology providers to delete student personal information in their possession when their contract with an educational institution terminates or within a "reasonable" time frame after such termination. Typically, such requirements are expressed in the contract so that all parties are clear about what happens to the student personal information when the contract is over. However, again, it is important to ensure that these provisions are properly articulated in any click-wrap agreements for classroom technologies.

Many states also allow students to retain their user-generated content in a personal account, including one they establish with the technology provider if the provider offers such features.

Access

Access requirements under state laws tend to fall on the side of restriction, as they do in most privacy laws. That is, ensuring that only those individuals and entities that need access to student personal information in order to perform a school function receive it.

This is quite similar to the FERPA requirements discussed in chapter 5, which establish that the educational institution must define what it considers to be a legitimate educational interest that may qualify an individual or entity as a school official and may provide school officials with only the personally identifiable student information in which they have a legitimate educational interest.

Many laws also reiterate existing parent access rights under FERPA, ensuring that parents may access, review, and request to amend or correct errors in their child's education record.

Some state laws also are designed to address more specific technology questions, such as ensuring that educational institutions do not compel students to provide their passwords for personal devices or social media accounts.

Use Restrictions

A critical difference between the federal and state student data privacy laws is the state focus on restricting data use for commercial purposes. It is very common to see state laws that specifically prohibit use of student personal information for the purpose of engaging in "targeted advertising" to students, and in some cases, to parents and teachers as well.

"Targeted advertising" is terminology that first appeared—but was not defined—in California's Student Online Personal Information Protection Act (SOPIPA). Under SOPIPA, technology providers covered by the law are prohibited from engaging in targeted advertising "when the targeting of the advertising is based upon any information, including covered information and persistent unique identifiers, that the operator has acquired because of the use of that operator's site, service or application."[4]

Since that time, a variety of states have copied this language. In some cases, the language has been refined to get closer to a clearer definition of what activities are and are not restricted.

For example, behaviorally targeted advertising clearly is prohibited.

Have you ever been surfing the internet and then been served ads that seem eerily appropriate for you? Online behavioral targeting is an efficient way for marketers to reach consumers who are most likely to engage with their brands. In a nutshell, online behavioral advertising works through the use of various tracking technologies that companies embed in websites and online services across the internet. They passively collect information about your browsing habits, then bundle that information to create a profile about who the marketer thinks you are based on your browsing data, sometimes aided by comparison to panel data. Advertising then can be served to you based on that profile.

From a marketer's perspective, the idea is that the advertising will be more appealing to you than untargeted advertising, because it will be for products and services that you are more likely to be interested in, based on who the advertisers think you are.

Whether this practice bothers you, or you like to receive ads that are more likely to be of interest to you, is a personal choice. However, it is not legal for young children under the Children's Online Privacy Protection Act (COPPA) and for students when the product was designed and marketed primarily for use in a K–12 environment. It is a commercial use of student data, which falls outside the realm of what is acceptable under a variety of state student data privacy laws, even with parental permission.

So, although the definition of targeted advertising is not always clear in state laws, we know enough to understand some of the boundaries.

It is also clear that, overall, states are concerned with the potential for student personal information to be used for marketing purposes. Concerns about marketing to young people are as old as the dawn of Saturday morning cartoons. Young children are a vulnerable population, afforded special regulatory protections, and there is longstanding regulation in the media sector intended to address the issue. However, it has reached the education sector for the first time in state student data privacy laws.

In addition, the restrictions in state student data privacy laws have moved beyond past concerns that were focused on marketing to children. In the case of states such as California, use of student data to market to adults, including parents and you, also is prohibited.

State laws also tend to prohibit the sale of student personal information, with exceptions made in the event that a technology provider is sold or undergoes another comparable change in ownership. In those cases, the laws account for the fact that the data may move with the sale, provided, however, that the data must remain subject to the previously existing data privacy policies. State laws also commonly restrict a technology provider's use of aggregated de-identified student information to purposes related to improving or developing its educational products and services, or demonstrating efficacy.

Transparency

Overarching all of the requirements is an interest in more or improved transparency about how student personal information is protected. A variety of state student data privacy laws require state educational agencies and institutions to develop data governance policies to help further protect the privacy of student data, and, in some cases, to develop uniform requirements for such protections across the state. Such policies usually are expected to be available publicly and easily accessible to parents.

In many cases, state educational agencies must document what data they collect from and about students, and educational institutions must make clear which technology providers they are working with. In certain states, the laws require that contracts with technology providers be made available publicly.

Still others take a different approach. New York State student data privacy law incorporates a requirement that educational institutions implement a "parents' bill of rights" explaining what data is collected and shared, how it is protected, and the limitations on its use. That bill of rights must be made publicly available on the educational institution's website and incorporated into contracts with technology providers.[5]

In addition, some of the laws reiterate legal requirements that exist across all sectors to ensure that material changes to privacy policies are not implemented without a technology provider first providing notice and obtaining prior consent.

Another key area of transparency involves notification in the event of unauthorized access to student personal information that constitutes a security breach. Some states have implemented requirements that, in addition to existing notification requirements to impacted individuals under the state breach notification laws, educational institutions must notify state authorities of data breaches within a defined time period.

Enforcement

Penalties for violating state student data privacy laws vary widely. Although already in effect, some of the laws are unfinished and include clauses requiring exploration and development of additional material to address unanswered questions, including enforcement.

For the laws that are complete, many include enforcement provisions directed at technology providers, with penalties being drawn from each state's existing business code. Those penalties often include monetary fines and, in extreme cases, could result in debarment.

However, educational institutions are not entirely in the clear, and, again, it's important to consult with your institution leadership so that you understand your role in supporting your institution's compliance with the state laws. Your institution should have policies in place to guide your actions in this regard. If you are able to read them again with fresh eyes, you may see the FIPPS concepts coming through there as well.

CHILDREN'S ONLINE PRIVACY
PROTECTION ACT (COPPA)[6]

COPPA does not apply to and is not enforced against educational institutions. However, it's important to understand it because, as with the other privacy laws, you may be making decisions about COPPA with the technology you bring into the classroom.

COPPA applies to operators of commercial websites and online services directed in whole or in part to children under age thirteen that collect, use, or disclose personal information from children under thirteen. It also applies to operators of general audience sites and services with knowledge that they are collecting, using, or disclosing personal information from children under thirteen, and to operators of sites and online services that have knowledge that they are collecting personal information directly from users of another site or service directed to children under thirteen.[7]

Proposals have been made over the years to apply certain protections in COPPA, such as those related to collection of geolocation data to children under the age of sixteen.[8] However, as of this writing, the requirement for compliance in the United States sits at under thirteen.

COPPA was written to address specific concerns about collection of personal information from young children for marketing purposes. It is enforced by the Federal Trade Commission (FTC) and state attorneys general against technology providers.

COPPA requires that technology providers obtain verifiable parental consent before collecting personal information from a child under the age of thirteen. However, when a contract exists between an educational institution and a technology provider, and when the personal information is to be collected only for the use and benefit of the school, and for no other commercial purpose, the technology provider may presume that the school's

TEXTBOX 6.1.   CONTRACTS

A contract is a contract is a contract.
Remember, when you "click to agree" to a technology provider's terms of use in a classroom app or website, you are signing a contract with the technology provider. As a result, when you click, you are affirming to the technology provider that if personal information will be collected from children under the age of thirteen, you or representatives at your educational institution have obtained the prior parental consents necessary under COPPA. You also are essentially determining that the technology provider has all of the necessary rights to obtain access to personally identifiable student information under FERPA and the contract you are agreeing to properly:

- Establishes your educational institution's direct control over the personally identifiable student information in the education record; and
- Articulates compliance with your state's student data privacy law and, where applicable, PPRA and COPPA.

It's a complex and significant responsibility. You also may or may not be authorized to sign contracts in your educational institution. This is discussed in more detail in chapter 7.

authorization for the collection of the students' personal information, illustrated by agreeing to the contract, is based on the school having obtained parental consent.

The operator is required to provide the educational institution with notice about its data collection, use, and disclosure practices in advance of any such agreement.[9] These notices should be evaluated by an authorized institution representative to help inform parental consent and to ensure that they are consistent with your educational institution's data privacy requirements.

Because you are not authorized to permit use of student personal information for commercial purposes, if the operator would like to do that, it is required to request permission directly from the parent or legal guardian. When such commercial use is restricted by state student data privacy laws, the state prohibition would rule.

In addition, COPPA requires that operators collect only the minimally required personal information necessary to provide a service or feature, not condition a child's participation in an activity or feature on providing information not necessary to fulfill that activity, provide reasonable security, and ensure that its third-party operators do the same.

Under COPPA, operators must allow parents to review the types or categories of personal information collected from their child. Parents must be given the opportunity to review the personal information collected from their child, refuse to allow the operator to make further use of their child's personal information, or require that the operator delete it. However, in such an event, the operator may revoke provision of the services to the child if the services cannot be provided without the child's personal information.

Parental rights under COPPA are important to understand. If a parent requests that an operator delete the child's personal information, such deletion may interfere with the education record when the technology is used in the classroom. To comply with FERPA, you'll need to maintain a copy of the education record, even as the parent is exercising their rights.

A good practice, then, is that you be able to ensure, through a process developed with your educational institution leadership and technology team, that your institution maintains a copy of the education record, even in the event that a parent requests that the technology provider delete their child's information.

COPPA is enforced against operators with financial penalties.[10] In addition, it is not uncommon for the FTC to require that violators delete the data they collected in violation of the law, to implement annual privacy training, and to submit to annual third-party compliance audits, often under multiyear consent decrees.

ADDITIONAL LAWS WITH PRIVACY IMPLICATIONS

There are other laws that often are not categorized as student data privacy laws, but that include considerations for privacy, some of which have implications for your classroom.

The Children's Internet Protection Act (CIPA)[11] is enforced by the Federal Communications Commission and applies to schools and libraries that receive discounts for internet access or internal connections through the E-rate program. In order to qualify for E-rate discounts, educational institutions and libraries must implement an internet safety policy that includes technology protections that block or filter internet access to pictures that are obscene, child pornography, or otherwise harmful to minors where the computer is accessed by minors.

That policy also must address safety and security of minors when using direct electronic communications such as e-mail and chat rooms, hacking, and other forms of unauthorized online access and unlawful activities by minors online, unauthorized disclosure, use and dissemination of personal information regarding minors, and measures restricting access by minors of materials deemed harmful to them.

In K–12 educational institutions, you probably are responsible for implementing a digital citizenship curriculum. This is a requirement of CIPA, which notes that educational institutions must educate their minor students about appropriate online behavior, including interacting on social media and in chat rooms, and cyberbullying awareness and response. Educational institution internet safety policies also must include monitoring of minor students' online activities. That, of course, requires data collection, and with that, consideration for the previously noted laws.

The National Student Lunch Act[12] makes clear that only individuals who need to know information about applications to the program in order to properly implement, record, or audit the program receive it. The privacy of those students eligible for free and reduced meal service is paramount.

In addition, it is possible that some of your educational institution's student data may be subject to the Health Insurance Portability and Accountability Act (HIPAA). HIPAA may apply if the educational institution is processing certain electronic transactions, applying to health plans, or any number of other transactional situations involving health data. However, for elementary and secondary schools, much of the student health information maintained by the institution that relates directly to the student, such as visits to the school nurse, commonly is subject to FERPA, not HIPAA.[13]

Exceptions exist, however, so as always, it's important to consult with your educational institution leadership and any existing policies and processes if you find yourself in a position to handle protected health information.

Under FERPA, because you are able to access only the information in which you have a legitimate educational interest, it is possible that you do not have access to a good deal of health information.

We've only just begun to explore how your behavior in the classroom might have a beneficial or adverse impact on your students' privacy. As much as is possible, refer to your educational institution's policies and procedures to guide you through their specific expectations.

NOTES AND NEXT STEPS

1. The laws are complex, sometimes contradictory, and not always easy to translate into action. However, it's important that you have at least a working knowledge of the key requirements. Do you have copies of your educational institution's policies and procedures that support your compliance with the laws? Are there policies and procedures that have not yet been developed that you think would be helpful? How could you work together with your leadership and technology team to put those in place?
2. How do you interact with technology providers that you bring into the classroom? Do they all have a legitimate educational interest in the student data they receive, and are they all qualified as school officials? How does your educational institution maintain direct control over the student personal information in the education records when you click to agree to the provider's terms of use? How does your institution ensure that technology that will be collecting personal information from students under age thirteen complies with COPPA? How is protection of sensitive student personal information, subject to PPRA, protected?
3. Are you able to articulate to parents how you work to support compliance with FERPA, PPRA, and state student data privacy laws in your classroom? How might you work with your technology team or educational institution leadership to develop more materials for parents to address their questions about the protection of student data privacy when using classroom technologies?

Chapter Seven

Bringing Technology into the Classroom

What do you do with all of that information about the laws? It can be understandably complex to try to translate the legal requirements into guidance for your everyday behavior. This is where your educational institution and its policies and procedures come in.

However, given the enormity of the task of properly protecting student data privacy, it is possible that your institution's data privacy compliance program is not yet robust enough to cover all of the policies and procedures you need to help guide your work. It is also possible that some of your institution's policies reiterate the laws but perhaps don't yet provide the action steps that bring the law to life for you in your daily work with student data.

You also now may better appreciate the issues that can arise when student personal information is shared in a manner that doesn't adhere to the laws and educational institution policies, or when it is used for purposes other than defined legitimate educational interests. These missteps can cause significant legal concerns for the institution. That is not to say that the responsibility for compliance sits solely on your shoulders, only that you are uniquely positioned to have a significant impact on your institution's compliance ecosystem.

One area in which this responsibility is fully present is in your work bringing technology into the classroom. In fact, nothing seems to worry your technology team more about your work than the prospect of you bringing apps and websites into the classroom without advance review for privacy and security issues.

It is a source of much discussion and hand wringing, informed by the complexities that these products can bring to the school environment. Nothing would please your technology team more than to put a sensible review process in place around classroom technologies before they're put in front of students, provided, of course, that they have the knowledge, resources, and your partnership to do so.

In the meantime, you may be looking at it through an entirely different lens.

A treasure trove of educational apps and websites is available, and no doubt you have found some gems that have proven to be truly effective for your students. New products are always coming into the marketplace, bringing new opportunities to reach your students in different ways. You've likely been able to find a combination of tools that engage and inspire your students in just the right ways; and with so many options to choose from, you're able to keep the material fresh. When you identify a tool that you think will be useful, you may move swiftly to leverage it in your classroom with the aim of setting your students up for success.

Why the stark differences in the way these classroom technologies are viewed? The short answer comes down to one word: risk. Your decisions about classroom technologies represent considerable potential to make the most significant impact on the privacy of your students, and where you may be taking the biggest gamble if you bring in products without putting them through a proper privacy and security review.

What Risks Exist When You Bring Technology into the Classroom?

First, let's be clear that this is not about stifling innovation or creating an environment in which you are unduly limited in the tools you can choose from to educate your students. This is simply about making savvy, well-informed, thoughtful decisions that protect you and your students. Doing so leads to better choices in the classroom, to the complete benefit of everyone involved.

Not all technology products you bring into the classroom are created equal. Many are built to properly protect student data in accordance with student data privacy laws, but some are not intended for use with students. Even when products are designed for use in the classroom, they may not meet your educational institution's requirements for privacy and security, which are in place to comply with the laws, to meet community expectations about how personal student information will be protected, and how technology will be leveraged for learning.

Bringing technology into the classroom without an initial privacy and security assessment means that you are taking on a variety of responsibilities that you may not be aware of and may not want. These include confirmation that:

- The product can and will operate in alignment with your educational institution's requirements for compliance with FERPA, your state student data privacy laws, and, where applicable, PPRA;

- Where applicable, the necessary prior parental consents for COPPA have been obtained;
- Your educational institution's policies for data protection and sharing, including qualifying the technology provider as a school official with a legitimate educational interest in the data it will receive, have been met;
- If you agree to terms of use, even if by click and not by written signature, you are authorized by your institution to sign such contracts and agree to everything represented in those terms;
- The student personal information that will be shared with the technology provider, whether gathered actively or passively, is appropriate and consistent with the legitimate educational interest;
- The terms you agree to in order to use the product appropriately express how the educational institution will maintain the required direct control over the student personal information; and
- The technology provider has agreed to use the student personal information only to serve the legitimate educational interest and will not use any de-identified student information in ways not permitted by your state laws.

There's more, but you get the idea. Are you prepared to take this on? Do you want to?

A better way to think about the technology you bring into the classroom involves working differently with your technology team and building a stronger partnership where everyone plays a role in ensuring that the technologies put in front of students are safe and appropriate for their use.

It may require slowing the pace with which you bring technology products into the classroom a bit, at least until a system is in place that not only meets your needs to leverage technology but also builds a partnership of shared responsibility with others in the educational institution to properly protect personal student information.

With that as the starting point, let's explore your role in discovering classroom technologies.

Discovery and Lesson Planning

Perhaps you searched a platform that reviews educational apps and websites and found a product you thought your students would enjoy and benefit from, or perhaps you learned about a new tool from a colleague. Maybe you were intrigued by what you learned about a technology product at an education conference, or by what you read in a recent education technology publication. These all certainly are useful paths for the initial discovery.

However, one thing should be clear: no one can know that a product is right for your students except you and your educational institution team, including your leadership and perhaps curriculum specialists. It is up to your institution to assess the product and determine whether it is actually educational, meets your curriculum needs, and its pedagogy aligns with your expectations.

If that determination hasn't been made, it stands to reason that the legitimate educational interest can't be assessed. Without that, sharing personal information with the technology provider becomes much more challenging, requiring prior written parental consent, but then only if legal compliance has been determined.

Once you have determined that a particular product is, indeed, a good candidate for classroom use based on the educational value, consider what it will add to the classroom experience. Is there something unique about this piece of technology that is not yet available in other technology products you're currently using? You wouldn't assign students numerous books to read that teach the same concepts and lessons over and over. The same is true for technology. What's additive about the material or method in the new product?

If the technology product does truly offer a unique value proposition, how you will use it? What lesson will you build around it, and how will you leverage it to meet the learning objectives in a new way?

Remember that bringing technology into the classroom is not the same as being innovative. Yes, there may be advances in technology that are noteworthy and that introduce novel techniques for engaging the learner. More than that, many classroom technologies adapt to a student's particular style, pace, and level of learning, making it possible and efficient to truly create and execute on individualized learning plans for all of your students.

Some products can measure how long it takes for a student to answer a question and idenfity whether or not they let the mouse hover in space, paused before selecting an answer or clicked quickly and confidently, all for the sake of presenting the next question that will challenge the student just enough to stretch as they solidify their knowledge of new ideas and concepts.

Even so, bringing this technology into the classroom is not innovative.

You are the innovator—not by bringing technology into the classroom, but by truly expanding on the potential of the technology and implementing it in the classroom in a way that is uniquely yours and suited to your students.

Instead of thinking of technology as innovation, start thinking of the work you do *with* technology as the place where the innovation comes into the classroom.

To truly innovate, then, you must read technology the way you do a book. You wouldn't assign a book for your students without reading it first. More than that, you might read it, take notes, build a lesson plan, consider which concepts and themes you will highlight, come up with essay topics or project assignments, create worksheets, and outline how you will direct class discussions.

Technology is no different. Before it comes into the classroom, be sure you have aligned it with specific educational aims and know how you will use it to fulfill those goals.

Is it Working?

When it comes to technology in the classroom, begin with the end in mind. With your educational objectives in hand, how will you measure efficacy? What does successful use of the technology product look like? How will you know that the educational aims have been met? Will you receive reports from the technology provider that demonstrate student progress? Will there be activities outside of the technology that you'll want students to complete in order to demonstrate their grasp of the material, or is progress within the product sufficient to demonstrate what the students have learned?

Consider how you'll know if the product is working as intended, and whether measuring efficacy is sufficiently convenient for you. If you'll need to pull reports from a product, perhaps request reports from the technology provider, log into the product and review each student's progress or assess whether the educational goals have been met through some other means, do you have the bandwidth to do that?

To Click or Not to Click?

Whenever you bring an app, a website, or some other technology product into the classroom, you are likely agreeing to the product terms of use or service and the privacy policy. You may do it—as many do—as part of the natural flow of signing up for the product, without even thinking about it. Do you read the terms and the privacy policy before you click the box to agree? If you're like most people, the answer is "no."

Whether in or out of the classroom, clicking to agree to online terms and privacy policies has become almost automatic in the modern age. We're asked to agree, and we do, sometimes without looking. Click and get past it so we can get into the app or website.

For legal reasons, sometimes companies require that we scroll through a long, complex, almost endless document before we're even permitted to click to agree. It's as if they're saying to us, "really, we want to be able to say that we encouraged you to read this, and so we're taking this step in the off chance that you might at least think about what you're agreeing to before you click." Yet still, so many scroll to the bottom, rushing past the agreement that's right in front of us, and click the box.

What if, instead of a box online to click, you were required to sign a written agreement on paper? What if it were your apartment or car lease agreement, employment contract or bank loan? Would your reaction to the paper in front of you be different than it is for something you click to agree to online? Would you review it carefully before signing? (I hope so!)

It may not feel like it, but that box you click is akin to you taking out a pen and signing your name to a paper contract. Whether it's words on a napkin, a long legal document, or a box online, a contract is a contract is a contract. It's not the media that makes it a contract; it's what's inside that counts. As long as it meets the legal standard for being a contractual agreement (which those terms you're clicking on will, unless the technology provider has done something very, very wrong), it's legally binding.

Why don't we read them? They're long. They're boring. They're often not easy to understand. They stand between us and what we want. However, by clicking to agree, you are effectively signing a contract, which may bind your educational institution to those terms.

Are you authorized to sign contracts for your school or district? If not, why are you doing it? If it were printed on paper instead of sitting online, would you sign your name to it? The next time you choose to click to agree, remember that you are signing it as if it were a paper contract.

Should someone else in your educational institution be signing them? Or could someone in your institution guide you about what types of online agreements you should and shouldn't sign and how to recognize what is and is not OK?

MAKING PRIVACY DECISIONS

What's in those terms and privacy policies anyway? Assuming that you've cleared up the questions about whether you are authorized to sign agreements as a school employee, how does signing these agreements impact your students' privacy? If you create an account in a product, how does signing the agreement impact your privacy?

It often comes down to what's in those agreements.

As we discussed in chapter 5, FERPA permits sharing of personally identifiable student information from the education record with a technology provider without prior written parental consent under limited circumstances. First, the technology provider must qualify as a school official with a legitimate educational interest in the student data. Do your classroom technology providers meet those standards as articulated in your institution's policies?

Assuming that is the case and that you're authorized to make that determination, how will you manage your educational institution's FERPA requirements in sharing the personal student information with the technology provider?

Remember that FERPA requires your educational institution to maintain "direct control" over the education record. The information you share about your students and the information your students share directly with the technology provider when using the product, including the work they may create in the product, usually is part of the education record. The direct control you need is managed through the contract agreement.

So that "click to agree" begins to take on even more significance, not only for you, but also for your students. Whatever is in those terms and that privacy policy is the company's legal representation about how it will operate, including what it will do with your students' personal information.

Consider the following:

- Do the terms articulate how the technology provider will remain under the direct control of your educational institution with respect to how it manages the education record?
- What does it do with the personal information, both yours and your students'?
- Where will the data be stored?
- Does the provider allow third parties access to the personal student information?
- If so, how does the technology provider manage third-party compliance with the privacy and security requirements for your students' personal information?
- What happens to the personal information after you finish using the product in the classroom?
- How will the technology provider ensure that the student personal information is properly secured, and when and how will the information be deleted?

Digging a bit more deeply, recall that the technology provider must use the personal student information only to support the legitimate educational interest. Assurances about what the technology provider will do with the personal student information should be articulated in the privacy policy. The privacy policy is also where you might find information about third parties operating in the product and how the technology provider manages their compliance.

No third-party tool or assessment can make this determination for your educational institution, and no tool will absolve your institution of the legal and reputational risks. If the product and the agreements aren't vetted in advance, how will you know if the technology provider is managing its legal requirements in accordance with your educational institution's policies?

This is important to know for all technologies that you bring into the classroom, but it takes on added importance for technologies that were not built for use in schools. Any number of applications in the marketplace are labeled "educational." However, that doesn't mean they meet any established educational standard, and it certainly doesn't mean that the technology provider created them with schools in mind.

Perhaps the product was meant to be educational for home use. Perhaps it was labeled as "educational" because technology providers know that parents will pay for products identified that way. Would the technology provider know it might be used in schools and, as such, have a responsibility to manage certain student data privacy requirements?

What Data Will You Share?

In previous chapters we discussed how FERPA mandates that you, as a school employee, receive access only to the data in which you have a legitimate educational interest. If you intend to share student personal information with a technology provider that has been designated as a school official, FERPA also requires that the educational institution ensure that the school official receive access only to the minimally required personal student information. Again, it is the privacy policy that should explain what personal information the technology provider will receive.

Is what it plans to and will collect only the information that is minimally required for the technology to work properly? Is the information that might be shared, although required for the technology to work properly, more than your educational institution is comfortable sharing with a technology provider, or deemed too sensitive to share?

It can be tempting to look at technology providers that do not require you or your students to enter obvious identifiers, such as names or e-mail addresses, and believe that no personal information is collected. However, remember that FERPA and other privacy regulations define personal information very broadly. Just because the technology provider doesn't know the students' name doesn't mean it is not collecting student personal information. A combination of indirect identifiers, including information collected passively as the user engages with the product, could be deemed personal information under the right circumstances.

That determination needs to be made by reviewing the privacy policy with consideration for what FERPA and your state student data privacy laws require, as well as COPPA if it's applicable. If that personal information is being gathered and an education record is being created, you need to know that it's being managed appropriately.

Is Everyone Old Enough?

You know that not all technology is meant for users of all ages, but let's discuss why those age limitations are in place. The most common age limitation you might see in a piece of technology that you'd like to use in the classroom is a note that the product is only meant for users age thirteen and over. This is the surest sign possible that the technology provider has not designed the product to be compliant with COPPA. This is the company's way of saying, "do not allow students under the age of thirteen to use this product. We do not want their data and are probably not equipped to protect it properly."

Heed the warning. Do not skirt the age limitations or bring technology into the classroom even if "most" of your students are the right age. That would be you deciding that it is OK for your students to use a piece of technology when the company that created it said that it cannot support the legal requirements to protect their privacy.

If the product is intended for use by children younger than thirteen, remember that COPPA requires the company to obtain verifiable parental consent before collecting any personal information from those children. If you click to agree to the terms, you are likely signaling to the company that you have managed all of the necessary parental permissions.

The FTC doesn't recommend that you manage these agreements under COPPA, but instead recommends that such decisions be handled by district leadership. In response to the question, "Who should provide consent—an individual teacher, the school administration, or the school district?," the FTC notes that "as a best practice, we recommend that schools or school districts decide whether a particular site's or service's information practices are appropriate, rather than delegating that decision to the teacher. Many schools have a process for assessing sites' and services' practices so that this task does not fall on individual teachers' shoulders."[1]

Although that guidance isn't binding, it's always worth heeding advice from the regulators. Note how their guidance supports you by removing a burden.

One additional, little-discussed implication of the age limitation is safety. When technology providers make products intended for young children, if they're doing it properly and are steeped in the knowledge of the special considerations and sensibilities that must be baked into such products, the products are designed with training wheels. That is, any features that children might use in a way that could get them into trouble from a safety perspective are created with all of the proper padding to keep them safe.

For example, a product that includes a social feature might be designed without the ability for children to connect with strangers—and everyone they do connect with is preapproved by a parent. A feature that permits students to collaborate might be available for you to review everything the students are doing to ensure that they are behaving online. A feature that permits children to "chat" online might be designed so that all comments are pre-moderated for appropriateness and to ensure that children are not able to share their personal information publicly.

When done properly, products for young children are designed to behave very differently than what we are used to seeing as adults. That is another reason why it's important to heed the age limitations on technology products. Privacy can be compromised, but safety might be as well if students are permitted to access technology that is not meant for them. Even when the technology is meant for young students, it's still important to ensure that any necessary safety measures are in place.

Make It a Team Effort

By now, you likely have a stronger understanding of some of the privacy risks that come with apps and websites that you may want to bring into the classroom. You don't need to go it alone when it comes to deciding on classroom technologies.

Your technology team also wants to ensure that the products you're bringing into the classroom are designed with the right privacy and security measures in mind. Those are necessary both to protect the student data and to protect your network from vulnerabilities that could impact not only your students' personal information, but also your personal information in the form of your employment records and payroll information that may be accessible via intruders on the network.

What adjustments can you make to the process? How can you build the right plan to keep leveraging classroom technologies and properly manage the compliance responsibilities surrounding the products? The answer is certainly not to go back to the age of pencil and paper for everything, nor is it to ignore the very real questions that your educational institution needs to answer about how a piece of technology meets its particular privacy and security requirements. The answer is balance.

By all means, keep looking for interesting, effective, novel ways to engage, educate, and inspire your students. Technology is a crucially important teaching and learning tool, and this is by no means intended to scare you off of it. However, bringing technology into the classroom is an important and complex decision. Why do it alone? Why take on all of the responsibility for meeting the requirements of the laws, your educational institution's policies, and community expectations? Why bear all of the risk when you may not be a compliance or technology expert and may not aspire to become one?

Your technology team is equally invested in ensuring that students are leveraging the best that technology has to offer. Partner on a new process that will support your efforts to bring technology products into the classroom. Now that you understand the requirements and responsibilities involved, you are better equipped to collaborate on a plan that will mitigate risk without compromising your ability to find new tools to work with.

At the same time, perhaps a process has been proposed in the past that just doesn't work for you. Perhaps it was too time-consuming, too onerous, and too disruptive. Or perhaps no one has proposed a process at all.

You can lead the change, or partner with your technology team to lead the change together. You have the need; they have some of the expertise to mitigate risk. Given your educational institution's existing resources, what would an ideal process look like if you were able to work nimbly through the landscape of available education apps and websites but had a trusted partnership that supported review of those products before anyone clicked to agree?

Given the sheer volume of apps and websites being used in most educational institutions, it might be nearly impossible to stop everything while existing classroom technologies are assessed. However, decisions should be made between you, your technology team, and educational institution leadership about how to best start building the process that changes the risk posture of the institution.

One option is to start building a library of approved technologies that will grow over time. The idea here is that you and your technology team work together to assess an array of technologies that already are being used in the classroom. Those become the first seeds of your technology library. Eventually, you might establish a process by which a reasonable selection of new technologies can be reviewed before you put them in the hands of students.

Start Small

Building a privacy program is a large and lofty project focused on ongoing improvement. It can be overwhelming to think about everything that entails, so don't try to tackle it all at once. Start where you are, and start small. Tiny, incremental improvements keep disruption to a minimum, build momentum, add up over time to impactful change, and give you the experience and confidence you need to engage around some of the larger issues.

Start by taking inventory of all of the websites, apps, and other connected technologies you use in the classroom this year. Does the number surprise you? Did you click to agree to all of the terms or privacy policies? Did you read all of those you agreed to? Looking back now, would you make that same decision today?

Meet with your technology team to determine how to approach the process of building a technology review program. For example, perhaps you might agree that you'll select the top five–ten products you deem to be "must-haves" for your classroom, or determine the ones that are used most often. Then ask your peers to do the same. Collect the top five or more products used in the classroom for each grade level. Which ones are on everyone's list? Which ones do you and your peers think are essential?

Once you've identified those, gather the products and print their privacy policies and terms of use. (Can't find a privacy policy? Remove it from your classroom immediately. That is a sure sign that the technology provider doesn't understand its minimal privacy responsibilities.) Ask your technology team to conduct a privacy and security review. Gather together to go through the results.

Everything that is subsequently approved from a privacy and security perspective would remain in the classroom. However, it is possible that your technology team will recommend that certain products no longer be permitted in the classroom.

Examples of some very valid reasons for that might include:

- The technology provider's privacy policy indicates that it engages in practices that would not be compliant with your state's student data privacy laws, your educational institution's FERPA obligations, or other privacy requirements;
- The product is intended for users older than those in your classroom;
- Your institution has no way to maintain direct control over its education records shared with the technology provider;
- Data shared with the technology provider will not be protected adequately;
- The product is configured in a manner that will put the security of the network at risk;
- Terms related to liability or other topics that the educational institution would have to agree to are untenable.

In short, the technology team likely will not say no unless the technology presents a meaningful risk to your educational institution and your students. Take time to explore other options and connect with other educators to see if they have found alternatives. If you consider the technology to be a "must-have" for your classroom, perhaps you and your technology team can reach out to the technology provider to see if it would be willing to make changes to meet your educational institution's requirements.

Some technology products likely may be used in the classroom only under certain conditions. For example, a particular product might be appropriate but only for users of a certain age, or certain features within a product may be acceptable but others create unacceptable risk to the educational institution. Another product that might be useful in delivering surveys involving sensitive information might require additional approval from administration, which may need to manage the PPRA consent process with parents before the product is implemented.

Finally, some products may be complex in ways that reach beyond your educational institution's resources to assess, so those may not be permitted. Either way, your institution should make an informed decision about use of technologies in the classroom, with full appreciation for the privacy laws and security protections that need to be in place to protect your student information.

When it comes to conditional approvals, be sure your technology team is specific about when and how you may use the technology. This will help to avoid confusion and errors in implementation.

The first few approved products become the kernel of a technology library. Once that's been established, develop a process for how technology products will be assessed in the future.

In such a process, would you be responsible for investigating the educational value and curriculum goals met by the technology, or would curriculum specialists do that work? What information might be needed in order to begin the vetting process, and who will be responsible for gathering it? Who will conduct the assessments? How many products can reasonably be assessed in any given year?

Depending on the size of your technology team, available bandwidth, and volume of classroom technologies you typically use each year, it may be possible or necessary for you to do some of the privacy and security reviews or some component of them.

If it does become necessary for you to do some of the work, bear in mind that you effectively sign off on privacy and security every time you click to agree to a technology provider's terms of use and privacy policy. Better to do that in an informed manner, with proper guidance and training, than without.

However, this should only be done if your educational institution's leadership and technology team agree to it. Of course, it's possible that for your institution, you are both the teacher and the technology team. Everyone's process might be different, depending on the available resources and organizational structure.

This is not to suggest that you become a privacy and security expert unless you want to, only that there may be simple steps you can take as a preliminary assessment that could help make any larger review process more efficient. For example, depending on the documentation available from your educational institution and available training and guidance, you may be able to confirm any or all of the following:

- No product already approved for use in your educational institution meets the same need;
- The technology provider has a publicly posted privacy policy and terms of use that can be reviewed;
- Based on the information in the terms of use and privacy policy, the product has no age restriction, or if it has, all of the students in your classroom meet the requirement;
- If the product is intended for use by students under age thirteen and will be collecting personal information from those students, the technology provider has submitted the required COPPA notice about its data collection, use, and disclosure practices for review;
- The technology provider qualifies as a school official with a legitimate educational interest in student information, will receive only the minimally required personal information, and that information is appropriate to share with school officials, based on your educational institution's documented policies;
- The personal information collected from and about your students will be used only to support the educational purpose;
- The technology provider has terms that state that it will not use student personal information for any commercial purpose;
- The manner in which your educational institution will maintain direct control over the education records shared with and created by the technology provider is consistent with your institution's documented requirements;
- The student personal information will be deleted in a time frame consistent with your state's student data privacy laws and your educational institution's documented requirements;
- The manner in which the technology provider will work with you and your educational institution to respond to requests from parents and eligible students to obtain access to information in their education record stored by the technology provider is clear and consistent with your institution's documented requirements.

This is not an all-encompassing privacy and security assessment. However, it is an example of how you might start going through the terms of use and privacy policy and identifying obvious indicators of a product worth considering for use in your classroom. By covering some of the basics, you may be able to help make the technology vetting process more efficient. At the least, you will start to better understand which products are worth pursuing and which carry a higher risk.

Your technology team may come up with more or different questions that should be easy to answer. They also can provide you with the information you need to identify the best answers to the above questions, taking you further along on your journey to "read" the technology before bringing it into the classroom.

It is by no means a perfect system. However, it does help to build fluency around appropriate technologies and supports the goal of providing a high standard of care for your students throughout their education while building a working partnership with your technology team to better support your classroom needs.

Districts of all sizes have implemented programs such as the one described above to help them better align their goals of supporting technology-enabled classrooms with keeping risk to the students and the educational institution as low as possible. It is not easy, and it will not happen overnight. Persist in the process, and you soon will have a robust library of tools to choose from while removing the full responsibility for the privacy and security of your students' personal information off of your shoulders. Along the way, you'll be co-creating the sensible and workable boundaries to help protect you, your students, and your educational institution.

The backlog of privacy and security review to complete may be large. This is a result of the way technology came into educational institutions in the first place: quickly, and without proper consideration for protecting student data privacy.

Conducting a privacy and security review of each piece of technology before it comes into the classroom takes time, energy, and commitment, just as it does to read books. It also takes a certain level of expertise and advance planning. You need to know your educational institution's data protection requirements, the technology provider's data protection practices, and the delta between them.

No quick-fix path leads through it. Each educational institution has to review the technology it brings into its buildings, just as you review books and other curriculum materials. No third party can tell you that a piece of technology complies with the laws, and implementation and interpretation of compliance in this arena belongs to each institution.

Getting started is the critical first step. Expect the work to be slow and challenging at first as the process ramps up. Take heart in knowing that once you are on the right path, it becomes much easier, doesn't result in undue restrictions or delays in bringing technology into the classroom, better protects your students' privacy, builds the trust and confidence of parents, and greatly improves the maturity of your technology practices.

NOTES AND NEXT STEPS

1. Bringing good technology into the classroom requires consideration for the learning objectives, privacy laws, cybersecurity, and the authority to sign a contract. Be sure you have covered all angles.
2. When it comes to classroom technology, don't underestimate the need to bring your creativity, guidance, and direction to the implementation plan for your students. Technology alone is not the lesson plan and it is not the innovation. That is up to you.
3. Don't go it alone. Partner with your technology team to put a process in place that will allow you to bring technology into the classroom safely, effectively, and in a manner that properly protects your students' privacy and builds the trust and confidence of your parent community.

Chapter Eight

Social Media

One need not look further than the daily news headlines to know that a number of privacy- and safety-related questions are swirling around social media. Your educational institution's leadership can determine if it will permit use of social media in the classrooms. However, if use is permitted, as with other technologies, it's important to understand the decisions you're making when you bring it into the classroom or use it to share information about your students and the responsibilities that go along with that.

We are not talking about a social media account that your educational institution may run to connect with parents that does not involve use or sharing of student personal information. Those often are used to communicate with parents about school events, schedules, and other noteworthy announcements. We trust that your educational institution has policies in place to ensure that those channels are private, are used responsibly, and that school employees are not sharing pictures or information about your students on those channels without proper authorization.

However, for your use in the classroom or to share information about your students, we can break down a few considerations to assess before diving in.

Age Appropriate

We use this term quite a bit when it comes to describing products for young people. Is it "age appropriate?" It can refer to a number of different things, including is it safe; is the content too mature; is it set up to comply with the applicable privacy laws; is there potential for harm, be it physical, mental, social, or emotional, from using this product? When it comes to social media, we're considering all of the above.

For K–12 students, when a social platform has not been designed or specifically designated by the operator for use in a K–12 educational setting, avoid it. When there's an age restriction on a product, including a social media platform, follow it. Few organizations would close their doors to people of a certain age without a compelling reason. Unless designed specifically for children under thirteen (and when it comes to social media, viable options have been few, if any), keep young children away.

Most social media platforms have been designed for what is referred to as a "general audience." That means adults and young people who are of an age that does not trigger privacy laws for children. Historically in the United States, that has been ages thirteen and older; however, as previously noted, that age may increase in the future. Overseas, in the EU and elsewhere, there is a range of ages at which parental involvement is required in consenting to privacy decisions; however, the EU has set a minimum threshold at thirteen.

The age limitation is in place for one reason: these platforms are not and do not intend to comply with COPPA. They do not need to and are not designed to. By permitting students under the age of thirteen to access social media in the classroom, you are compromising your students' privacy.

Although that should be sufficient to answer the question about why the age limitations are in place and why they are important, the safety considerations of products not intended for children are strongest when it comes to social media. Platforms built for children may include content that has been carefully curated to be age appropriate, connections with other individuals on the product often are done with parental involvement and approval, and communication within the product between users is limited and, ideally, carefully moderated to protect users from predators and others who may be intent on harm, be it through bullying or other means.

Products intended for a general audience have not been built with those considerations in mind. There may be some moderation of comments after they've been made, or an attempt to keep the platform free of malice, but operating in the general audience ecosystem is, by its very nature, a completely different exercise than operating in one meant for students.

EDUCATIONAL PURPOSE

Assuming that your students are old enough to access social media platforms, what is the educational purpose for using social media in the classroom? Recall from our review of FERPA that unless one of the other noted exceptions applies, you may not permit sharing of student data with a technology provider without prior written parental consent if the provider does not have a legitimate educational interest in the data and meet your educational institution's criteria for a school official.

Because social media platforms were not built for use in educational institutions, what case must be made in your institution for the technology provider to qualify as a school official with a legitimate educational interest in the student personal information?

If you are sharing the information under the directory information exception of FERPA, has all of the information you will share been properly designated as directory information, and have you confirmed that no parents have opted their child out of sharing such information? If your educational institution has a limited release directory information policy, has social media use been disclosed as an acceptable use?

Also bear in mind that when not designed for use in educational institutions, social media platforms leverage their user data for commercial purposes. Typically, they glean information from their users to determine what advertising would be most effective for the individual, and use that information to support their advertiser community. If you do not have the necessary written consents, or if your state's student data privacy laws prohibit use of student information for targeted advertising purposes, sharing student information on those social media platforms also would be prohibited.

As a result, regardless of the student's age, it could be difficult to find a legal use case for social media platforms in the classroom when they are not specifically designed for that purpose, in alignment with all of the applicable student data privacy laws.

If you can find a use case that is educational, consistent with your educational institution's technology use policies and that involves a platform or a portion of a platform that is specifically designed for use in schools, in compliance with the student data privacy laws, be sure to check the privacy configurations.

Most social platforms allow users some control over how public or private their information is. For students, ensure that the default setting is private, such that information is shared only in the way that you have determined is appropriate for your students. For most, that might mean the most restrictive settings, in a closed group, such that their information is only available to be shared with others in your classroom.

While you're at it, check the privacy settings on your personal social media pages. Be a good role model to your students (and perhaps keep your personal life away from their curious minds) by ensuring that you are not sharing your information publicly unless it is a deliberate choice.

Show, Tell, and Display

In some cases, you may choose simply to display information from a social networking platform to your students and not ask that they use the site. For example, you may want to play a video in the classroom that is only housed on a site intended for a general audience. This type of display doesn't have privacy implications for your students' personal information if you are the one operating the machine on which the material is displayed and you are not otherwise permitting any sharing of your students' information.

You may, however, have had the experience of having these types of sites blocked by your technology team for purposes related to CIPA, network bandwidth, or security. Again, partner with your technology team to see where you can create workable processes so that you can operate seamlessly in the classroom with the technologies you need, or work together to find suitable alternatives.

A word of caution: Avoid talking about your students on social media or posting their pictures unless:

- It is expressly permitted under your educational institution's policies;
- You are authorized with written consent from each parent to do so; and
- You are posting to a group that you have confirmed is private and open only to parents of the children about whom you are posting.

It's very common for educators to post pictures of their students on social media platforms, always with the best of intentions: to showcase how the students are engaged, to give parents a peek into the classroom. Also common is to post pictures of assignments or humorous test answers without redacting the student's personal information. Far too often, these posts are done without permission from the parent, and in a public-facing area.

Why does this matter?

First, consider the legal authority to share the student data on a public platform. Is the information, which perhaps includes student names or photos designated as "directory information" under FERPA by your educational institution? If so, has your leadership determined that sharing on social media is an acceptable use of that personal information?

Next, remember that by sharing on social media, whether in a private group or not, the information will become subject to the social media platform's privacy policy. Is that policy protective enough for your students' personal information, or are there risks that make the data exposure unpalatable or uncompliant?

Remember, too, that sharing on social media outside of a closed group means that anyone accessing the platform can see the information. A photo of a student tells us a lot: appearance, approximate age, grade level (usually based on information displayed or readily available via your profile), and school. That presents potential safety issues for your student. Why take that risk?

If you do have permission from parents to share student information in a closed group on social media, curate your group carefully. Once a child has moved on from your classroom, be sure that the parent's access to your group is removed as well. Ensure that you or an authorized individual in your educational institution is able to maintain a private group that includes only the parents of your active students, and only when the parent has provided you with permission to share their child's information in that way.

Always follow your educational institution's policies and use your best discretion when deciding what information to post. Be certain that it is information that parents are comfortable sharing with other parents in the class.

We commonly see teachers sharing their student information another way: posting videos online. It's become common practice for educators to record students delivering the morning announcements and post them on video sharing sites. At this point, I imagine that you are starting to rethink that practice, or at least to push it through the lens of the many different privacy laws that might apply, as well as the safety risks.

In addition to everything we've discussed about social media platforms, remember that students like to see themselves. If you're recording them and posting those videos online, even if you're doing it with parental permission and in a closed group to protect their safety, what's happening with their data privacy?

As with social media platforms, not all popular video viewing and video sharing platforms have been designed with children in mind. Unless specifically designed for use in educational institutions, they usually operate as general audience platforms for which the protections of COPPA don't apply. If the product was not designed for use in the classroom, the various student data privacy laws also don't apply, which means the student data is not being managed in a way that supports your educational institution's compliance with FERPA or in compliance with state student data privacy laws.

The practice raises a very important question: Why post information about students on platforms that are not meant for them, in ways that would appeal to them, when going to those platforms would be detrimental to your students' privacy and your responsibilities to your educational institution? Could you do something else equally engaging that serves the same purpose but uses compliant technology?

When it comes to maintaining the privacy of student personal information, you're one of the strongest links in the chain in protecting your students and your educational institution. Be sure that the decisions you make are done with eyes wide open and well-informed by the legal and your educational institution's policy requirements.

If your institution does not yet have a policy for this type of social media use, what would a responsible policy look like? Can you propose one? Would you ban the practice in your educational institution, or carve out conditions and requirements that must be met in order to leverage social platforms responsibly? What policy would you propose if you were responsible for your students' privacy and educational institution's legal compliance? Before you ask to use a particular platform, can you envision a policy that addresses all of the privacy requirements?

NOTES AND NEXT STEPS

1. Access to some social media platforms may be prohibited in your educational institution due to CIPA or other privacy law requirements. Are you fluent in those requirements and any other limitations on use of those platforms in your classroom?
2. Provided that use of social media platforms is acceptable under your educational institution's policies, before permitting your students to use social media, be sure that they meet the minimum age requirements and have a well-defined curriculum goal that can't be achieved without it. Have the platform vetted to ensure that it can be used in a manner that is consistent with student data privacy law requirements.
3. Don't share any information about your students on social media without advance written consent from the parents. Be mindful of both privacy and safety concerns with social media platforms, and use the strictest privacy settings. If you are sharing with a closed parent group, manage participants carefully to ensure that only those authorized are able to access the group.

Chapter Nine

New Technologies

It seems that almost every day a new technology is brought to market, or a new application is introduced for an existing product. The possibilities are endless: virtual reality, artificial intelligence, facial recognition, and whatever comes next. Most of these products have not been designed with your students, student data privacy laws, or educators in mind. However, given that they're often introduced to the market with a good deal of excitement and promise, these products commonly find their way into the classroom anyway.

When the education technology conference you're attending includes sessions on how to use a new technology in the classroom, or when an education technology publication features educators from across the country talking about how the product is revolutionizing their classroom management or that students are engaged like never before, it's tempting to jump on the bandwagon—and to do it quickly.

The question is: How do you know what technology is appropriate for use in your classroom and what products are likely to jeopardize your students' privacy and your educational institution's legal compliance?

Almost every new technology could have *some* educational benefit and could be used to engage and inspire students in new ways. However, how are you to decide what new technologies to bring into your classroom without having your decision put your students' data privacy and your educational institution's compliance with federal and state laws at risk? How might you cut through the noise that tends to accompany such products and focus on properly assessing the technologies, starting with determining the benefits and risks to your students?

It's hard not to get swept up in the tide of enthusiasm for new technologies, especially when the enthusiasm is coming from your peers and other trusted sources of information. However, you now are equipped with more information than many about your data privacy responsibilities. By adding that to the mix, you are better prepared to make more informed, deliberate decisions. The next time everyone's talking about a new technology on the scene, take a moment to consider the source of the information and the substance of the discussion in the context of what you know about student data privacy requirements.

Where did you hear about the product? Did word come from a knowledgeable peer, an education publication, or an education conference session? What is their interest in promoting the technology? If you read about a product in a publication, does it seem as if it is written from a press release, or an analysis of the product from all angles? Does the article focus on when the product will be available, the benefits, and various uses? Or is the piece more balanced, perhaps discussing the benefits but also some challenges that may have come up in introducing it in the classroom?

What's the focus of the information you're relying on? Is your source considering only the novelty of the product? What, if anything, is mentioned about the legality or appropriateness of the technology in the classroom? Does the information include any point of view from privacy experts or educational institution technologists focused on security? What are the privacy questions you might ask after reading the piece?

Absence of a privacy discussion doesn't mean the product can't be used in a compliant manner, nor does it mean that it can. However, try to avoid being swept up in the enthusiasm of an article that perhaps was not focusing on the complexities of student data privacy requirements or general implementation challenges.

It's not uncommon to see education conference sessions focused on the utility of a new technology in the classroom. However, it's quite rare to hear questions about privacy laws addressed in those sessions. The next time you're in one of those sessions, consider the following:

- Is the product designed for use in schools? If not, what criteria were used to determine that it was acceptable for the presenter to use it in the educational institution? Does anything in the terms of service or privacy policy indicate that using the product in the classroom would be in compliance with FERPA, PPRA, or your state's student data privacy laws?
- What's the focus on the presentation? Is it primarily a feature-based discussion explaining the ways the product can best be used with students? Is there any discussion of how the product might be used in compliance with privacy laws or the necessary security configurations?
- How is efficacy of the product measured?

- What student personal information will be collected? Will it be student names, images, voices, or something else?
- What is the legitimate educational interest that the technology provider might have in any student personal information it will receive?
- What does the technology provider do with the student personal information? Is that use case consistent with the legitimate educational interest defined by your educational institution? Would the technology provider qualify as a school official?
- How would you maintain direct control over the education record if you used this product in your classroom? How would you ensure that the student personal information would be deleted when no longer needed or upon request?
- If a parent or eligible student were to exercise their FERPA rights and request a copy of the student's education record, how would the technology provider help to facilitate providing your educational institution with that information?
- According to the technology provider's terms, what are the age requirements for using the technology? Are your students old enough to use it in compliance with those terms?
- Bear in mind that if the product was not designed for use in schools and the technology provider doesn't know its product is being used in your classroom, it may not be required to comply with your state's student data privacy laws. In that case, are you prepared to determine that the use will not compromise your students' privacy?
- Do you have enough information to discuss the product with your technology team? If the product would provide content to students, as is the case with many artificial intelligence products, is your technology team able to set it up to be filtered properly on the network in compliance with your educational institution's CIPA requirements?

It's seems unfair that education conferences and publications regularly promote new technologies for use in the classroom, even when the products aren't designed for it. There is a rush to bring in whatever is new and different in an attempt to engage students. But new, different, and engaging does not mean it's educational, beneficial, or appropriate. It also doesn't mean that it can be used in compliance with the laws. All too often, the promotion you're seeing is not informed by data privacy requirements.

Be a leader, not a follower, and resist the urge to go with the flow. When new technology hits the market, remember to read it like a book. Consider whether it is truly differentiated from existing and available technologies to the extent that it warrants a privacy and security review. If it does, assess the educational benefit and how you would integrate it into your lesson plans. Then partner with your technology team in alignment with your established process on a request to conduct privacy and security diligence.

Also, remember that if the technology provider indicates either formally in documentation or informally in quiet conversation that it does not intend the product to be used in the classroom, avoid it. Technology providers don't make those representations lightly. If the technology provider indicates that the product is not intended for use in schools, it likely is saying that the product is not designed to be used in compliance with student data privacy laws.

NOTES AND NEXT STEPS

1. When considering whether a new technology is a good fit for your classroom, ignore the hype. Be a savvy consumer and ask the hard questions. Is the product intended for use in the classroom? Can it be used safely and effectively with your students? Can it be run securely on your educational institution's network? Can what you've learned about the product's privacy practices and efficacy be verified?
2. How will use of the new technology enhance your teaching methods or the way your students learn? What specific benefits will it provide, and how will you ensure that it is implemented in a manner that properly protects your students' privacy?
3. Will you be able to explain the educational benefits, privacy protections, and curriculum goals to parents? What other questions might you anticipate about the new technology, and what information might you need to respond to them?

Chapter Ten

Sharing Is Not Caring

When you're connecting with parents about their child's performance in your classroom, have you ever, out of the goodness of your heart, also checked to see how their other children might be doing in other classes? It's a kind thing to do for a parent. It comes from the best of intentions. Unfortunately, it may also be the wrong thing to do.

Sharing student information is part of the fabric of how educational institutions operate. Sometimes that information sharing is necessary; however, when we become too loose in our disclosure, we also loosen our grip on our responsibilities.

Stories abound about well-meaning educators looking at the education record of students whom they do not directly support. Sometimes it's to answer questions for the parent, sometimes it's to try to help the student. In still other cases, information has been accessed to check on the background of the boy that the educator's child is dating, or to "just see how the kids in the neighborhood are doing." That's not what the information is there for. Such access is neither legal nor justifiable.

It is, however, human nature. Whether in a social context or a work context, people will talk, usually about other people. Some avoid the chatter, others want to be the first to know, and many, at the very least, want not to be the last to know. It's natural to want to know as much as possible about your students. After all, they are in your care for so long almost every day, and your job is nothing less than to help them get the foundational education they need to go out into the world prepared for success. Sometimes the more you know, the more you can help them.

Information is a currency and a commodity. It is also a liability. The responsibility to protect your students' privacy is quite clear. However,

81

the natural tendency often is to gather as much information as possible about them.

Practice good data privacy practices (and comply with the laws) by limiting your access to student personal information to only those students for whom you have an educational responsibility for the educational purpose. When it's out of reach, your students and their personal information are better protected, and so are you.

Before you access information about the students you do support, ask yourself what educational purpose it serves. How is your access to that information supporting the student's learning? If access to that information was taken away, would it prohibit you from doing your work? The answer may be "yes," in which case, it's probably a good sign that the information you're looking for may be permissible under the laws.

If the answer is "no" or "maybe," it's worth additional exploration. How would not having access to the information impede your ability to support that student? Could you accomplish your goals without the information? The less you access information that is extraneous to the task you're engaged in, the better.

This is not to suggest that you don't need robust volumes of data at your fingertips in order to best support your students and succeed in your role. You do. But it is worth considering whether information you have access to is truly necessary. That's where the risk lies. FERPA requires that school officials only have access to information in which they have a legitimate educational interest. Beyond that, unnecessary access to data is both a privacy and security risk. Avoid it.

Sharing limitations extend to sharing with other teachers as well. Check with your administration to be sure you are clear about the boundaries around sharing student personal information within your organization. Often there is a legitimate educational purpose for the work, sometimes to collaborate around student support and sometimes to assess some of the best teaching practices. However, if you're unclear on what your educational institution's policies are in this area, you may be taking unnecessary risks.

Remember that when sharing lesson plans and classroom practices, often it is not necessary to share the student personal information, and in some cases it's not appropriate to do so. Be empowered around the boundaries so that you can maneuver effectively within them.

If a policy doesn't exist at your educational institution, it's another opportunity for you to partner with leadership and your technology team to develop one that takes into consideration your data access needs. Why not propose sensible, holistic rules that consider privacy, security, and what you need to be effective? After all, your voice should be heard on such policy matters as much as that of other educational institution stakeholders.

When you do share student personal information for approved purposes within your institution, how do you share it? Do you use specifically designated, secure files to transfer information? Do you use online collaboration platforms and documents?

Great tools are available for securely sharing information, cocreating materials, and maintaining access to the information. However, as your technology team likely has told you, not all data is meant to be shared on all platforms. They simply are not all capable of or not configured properly to keep such information secure.

Bear in mind that as part of your educational institution's requirements to protect student personal information, your technology team likely has gone through an exercise of determining which data is most sensitive and how that data needs to be secured. Once that work was completed, they would have determined what file formats and platforms could be used to transfer the data while maintaining the right levels of security.

This can be rather painstaking work. It involves gathering all of the data fields your educational institution collects, and for each data element, determining how sensitive that data might be. Usually the criteria for determining sensitivity are based on the risk of harm if there were an unauthorized release of the data.

For example, your Social Security number, financial information, and health information should be categorized as highly sensitive, just as that data would be for your students and their parents. If such data were released, it has high potential to cause tangible harm. Your educational institution likely has classified other types of personal information as highly sensitive.

Your technology team also would have classified additional data elements as moderately sensitive; and still some data, such as student names, might not be very sensitive at all, perhaps indicating that it could be released to the public if there were a request for it.

Once all of the personal information was classified in accordance with sensitivity and risk, your technology team likely went through the exercise of determining how it should be protected. Obviously, they'd want to ensure that the strongest protections were in place for the most sensitive data. This would include limitations on access to only those employees with a "need to know" in order to do their work. Additional administrative safeguards, as well as complex and sometimes costly technical and physical safeguards, also would be put in place to help ensure that it remained protected from unauthorized access.

This same work would have been done for data of differing sensitivity levels. This is often foundational work your technology team would have to do to ensure that your and your students' personal information was in the right systems, accessible to the right people, both available to those who need it and secure from those who should not have access to it.

In order for the data to remain secure, this classification and protection need to remain in place no matter where the data is and no matter how it travels. Your technology team also may have determined how it could be securely transmitted (if at all) and on what platforms. Sometimes the security level is due to the platform itself, and sometimes it's how we have to behave in relation to configuring and operating the platform that impacts the security.

For example, when sensitive personal information is transmitted via e-mail, the necessary protections may be broken. E-mail is extremely vulnerable to risk through our behavior, be it falling for phishing, use of unsecure Wi-Fi, or other actions. It then becomes, for all practical purposes, impossible to track where the data ends up once it's been transmitted via e-mail. It's out of our control, and the intended recipient can pass it on without our knowledge. It's an untenable situation from both privacy and security perspectives.

As such, your educational institution likely has policies that clarify how e-mail may and may not be used. These policies likely prohibit or restrict sharing student personal information via e-mail, and perhaps also prohibit use of your personal e-mail for your school work. These policies are part of the safeguards in place to protect the personal information. They're there to protect the network, your information, and that of your students.

Another common practice is to use online collaboration tools to partner with colleagues on lesson plans. Technology providers have made it so easy and seamless to implement these collaboration tools that it's easy to forget that we have to be savvy about what data we place on them and how we manage it. Bad privacy habits with collaboration tools are common.

For example, assuming that you have a need to share student personal information with other school officials authorized to have access to that information, most users of collaboration tools fail to delete the information once the collaboration project is over. It often remains available, accessible to all of the collaborators, stored on the technology provider platform, long after the project has ended. Over time, the fact that the information remains available on the platform is often forgotten, and what we don't remember, we can't properly protect.

When using collaboration tools, to ensure that your experience is effective for you while also protective of your students, consider the following:

- Use only those collaboration tools that have been approved by your technology team for your intended purpose and data sharing.

- What, if any, personal data is required to achieve your goal? Are you practicing good data minimization practices, or are you sharing unnecessary personal information? Can you achieve your goals by only sharing de-identified student data?
- With whom are you sharing the information? Have you determined that everyone is authorized to have access to personal information you'll need to share?
- How will you protect the information? Will accessing the information require a password, a special invitation, or other authorization? Will everyone with access be able to view the information, change it, or just comment on it? What practices will be in place to maintain the integrity of the data?
- How long will the information remain on the platform? Do you have an expiration date in mind for the materials you're sharing? Do you know before you share the information how you'll revoke access and remove it from the platform when your project is finished?

A bit of planning at the outset will help ensure that you're properly protecting the data. What's more, after you've worked through the process once and have learned the simple protocols, it easily can become a turnkey part of your process.

You Can't Take It with You

As you grow in your career, you no doubt want to keep records of some of the great work you've done. Lesson plans you've created that were particularly effective, techniques you've used to reach students who needed your support the most, and examples of how you've improved your teaching practice over time are just part of the record of your work that you may want to maintain.

Recording your successes is important to your career growth and improvement. Having tangible evidence of where and how you've been most effective also will allow you to leverage that for the benefit of your future students. It's natural that you'd want to keep personal records of that work and be able to bring it with you if you move to a new educational institution.

However, within your educational institution your lesson plans often are entangled with student personal information. As you now know, that information cannot make it into your personal records or devices, or move with you to a new institution. That would conflict with FERPA and possibly your state's student data privacy laws.

Here's another area where working with your technology team can be particularly helpful. Your leadership may permit you to keep copies of a variety of materials once the student personal information has been removed.

Accomplishing that will take work. It would be nearly impossible to fully separate the record from its association with your educational institution. That fact, combined with a small sample size of students, may render it very difficult to ensure that the data is not identifiable. However, with careful attention to detail, it should be possible to preserve the materials and methods you created, as well as metrics about how your students improved through your implementation, without compromising student privacy.

In partnership with your technology team, consider whether they can support development of standard methodology for de-identifying lesson plans, teaching tools, and success metrics. With an established process, it may be possible to preserve the information you want in a manner that is efficient and effective. Doing so also will mitigate the risk by ensuring that you do not end up with student personal information on your personal devices, in your home, or carried with you to another educational institution.

No one is arguing that data often needs to be shared in order to be of use at all. Working in isolation is not only unrealistic, but it's often counterproductive to positive outcomes. When you do share information, whether with parents, colleagues, or as part of your own reference guide, do so thoughtfully and in strict alignment with your educational institution's policies and processes.

NOTES AND NEXT STEPS

1. By all means, collaborate with your colleagues to improve your practices and support better student outcomes. However, respect platform limitations mandated by your educational institution. Restrict access to any shared folders to a limited distribution of those who need to have such access and are authorized to do so. Avoid using student personal information wherever possible, and when the project is over, delete the data from the shared platform.

2. It's natural that you may want to keep a personal record of your best work to support student success in the future. Map out a plan with your technology team to ensure that any student personal information is removed from those records before you move it out of the educational institution's platforms.

3. Unless your educational institution's policies authorize you to access and share information about students not in your class, keep your conversations with parents limited to the child you teach. Have contact information for educators of a parent's other children handy in the event that a parent asks you to gather information about their children not connected to your classroom.

Chapter Eleven

Security Simplified

Hardly a week passes without reading about a new data security incident. Sometimes the news is quite dramatic, and it seems as if no industry sector has been left unscathed. Unfortunately, when it comes to securing our personal information, no system is airtight, and despite the attention being paid to cybersecurity, the incidents keep piling up.

We see the headlines, but we don't often see the work an organization needs to do to clean up in the aftermath of a data security breach. We know it must be a big project, but what's really happening behind the scenes?

Massive disruption often is the short answer. In the immediate hours following discovery of a data security incident, technology teams work to identify where and why some potential unauthorized access to personal information occurred, and what type of data is being released. Top priorities include stopping the flow of data out of the organization as quickly as possible.

Eventually, attention turns to determining exactly what data was released, how much, to whom it belonged, where it ended up, and why. Laws are consulted, sometimes forensics firms and law enforcement are engaged, and communications teams may be mobilized. As the specifics of the situation emerge, attention turns to providing any legally required notice to those who were impacted and explaining to the community what happened. Regulators may need to be notified as well.

All the while, work is going on within the organization to build a road map for the future to ensure that the same situation doesn't happen again.

This all unfolds in a matter of days, but the cleanup in the aftermath can be a long, expensive, and difficult process. The nature of the particular security incident may be such that systems need to be rebuilt, policies and procedures implemented, and at times, the entire organizational culture changed to focus more rigorous attention on data protection.

No matter how the situation unfolds, it can be a tense time for any organization.

The education sector is no stranger to security incidents. A good deal of attention is paid to the state of cybersecurity at higher education institutions, where potential financial gain and advantages of getting insight into ongoing research can be motivating factors for hackers.

In the K–12 sector, potential financial gain is to be found via theft of data, such as students' Social Security numbers and your payroll information. In both higher education and K–12, sometimes the potential financial gain to be had is through ransomware, essentially holding a server hostage, or by duping unsuspecting employees into fulfilling financial requests for hackers posing as supervisors.

In one particularly disturbing case, hackers infiltrated the server for Columbia Falls School District 6 in Montana, accessing student, alumni, and employee records. The perpetrators then sent a letter to the district requesting a ransom of digital currency in exchange for not releasing personal information about students, teachers, and other school employees.[1] The letter was so disturbing that the district closed for three days, disrupting the lives and education of approximately fifteen thousand students.[2]

In another example, two twelve-year-old students at Rochester Community Schools in Michigan found a username and password that had been left on a sticky note next to a computer in their middle-school library. Curious, they logged on and found student and teacher information, including passwords, lesson plans, and exams. They subsequently obtained access to the educational institution's security cameras by yet again accessing a username and password that had been posted on a sticky note on the security guard's laptop.[3] The students were expelled and found themselves the target of a criminal investigation, although no evidence suggests that they did anything but look at the information they were able to access.[4]

In 2018, Chicago Public Schools reported a few different data security incidents, including one in which an employee sent an e-mail to more than thirty-seven hundred families that included a link to a file with information on all of the intended recipients' names, e-mail addresses, phone numbers, and student IDs.[5] The district closed out the year with an announcement that settings on a Google Drive folder had been misconfigured, resulting in improper disclosure of employee ratings, student grades, and standardized test scores, race, special education status, and more.[6]

In San Diego, phishing e-mails were used to gain access to login credentials for approximately fifty employees, which then were used to access files that contained sensitive information concerning more than five hundred thousand employees and students.[7] The result was that employee and student data, including names, addresses, health information, Social Security numbers, employee benefits details, payroll and banking data, employee and student emergency contact information, and more was able to be viewed or copied over the course of eleven months.[8]

Given all that's happening, it is often a question of not *if* your educational institution will experience a security incident, but *when*.

It can be tempting to look at all of industry and think that if the most well-resourced and technologically sophisticated companies can be breached, how can we stand a chance? That line of thinking, while tempting, ignores one of the most common causes of security incidents and the first line of defense against them: people.

The truth about many security incidents, and the common theme in all of the situations we've discussed here so far, is that they often are caused—or at least made possible—by our behavior. The technology doesn't fail to work. We do. In the case of educational institution security breaches, although the vast majority are the work of an outsider,[9] often an employee's mistake or lack of knowledge makes a security incident possible.[10]

Although it may not be apparent at first glance, the fact that so many security incidents are permitted by our behavior is good news. It means that a large number of these situations are entirely preventable. Many security incidents, and the resulting harm to you and your coworkers, students, parents, and the educational institution infrastructure, can be avoided.

Every employee plays a role in ensuring that the school system network, student data, and your data remain protected. Any weak link in the chain can result in harm. Mistakes and accidents can and will happen. However, by creating a strong foundation of simple, security-conscious behaviors, those situations will be few and far between, and the impacts may be lessened significantly.

It may be hard to believe that simple behavior changes can prevent catastrophic security incidents, but sometimes that's all it takes. Even more good news is that taking these steps doesn't need to involve becoming an expert in security or technology, nor does it require that you understand any of the security-related jargon and acronyms sometimes used by technology teams.

All it requires is that we do things differently.

Doing things differently begins, of course, with knowledge. Using the simplest terms, let's look at some of the most common ways in which hackers gain access to systems and how your behavior can prevent it.

Table 11.1. Mitigating Risk of Security Incidents

Common Intrusion Tactics in Education[1]	How to Help Prevent the Issue

Malware:

As the name suggests, malware is "malicious software." Often it is designed to gain unauthorized access to your computer and do damage, be it stealing your data, taking control of certain programs, or otherwise wreaking havoc on how your device functions.

Malware makes its way onto devices through a number of different avenues, but many are triggered by how we behave. For example, if you click on a suspicious web link or an attachment in an e-mail or a text message, or if you click on infected ads online, if you visit websites that have been compromised, or if you download compromised materials onto your computer, you may be opening the door to malware.

Preventive measures include:

- Only access credible websites and online services that are consistent with your educational institution's policies;
- Don't circumvent filters that your technology team has put in place to access restricted websites;
- Review e-mail and text messages carefully before clicking on links in the messages or downloading attachments. Is it from someone you recognize? Does it contain unusual typographical errors or poor grammar? Were you expecting to receive the link or attachment from this person? Is something fishy about it that you just can't pinpoint? These are all good signs that you should not click. Delete the message or alert your technology team, who can help to confirm whether the message is problematic.
- Use only approved devices in your educational institution, configured by your technology team with adequate security to help prevent a number of issues, including what is referred to as "drive-by malware." Drive-by malware is installed on your device when you visit an infected website or ad banner. You may have no way to tell that the online material is infected, but a properly configured device with up-to-date protections can block a number of bad actors.
- Avoid using public Wi-Fi. It's not secure and can be a vehicle for malware and general snooping on your machine.

Ransomware:

Malware that is designed to encrypt data files and keep them out of reach until a ransom has been paid is referred to as ransomware. With ransomware, once the files have been encrypted, the only way to access them is either to recover a viable backup that the institution has available or pay a ransom.

Simply put, everything you do to prevent malware also will help prevent ransomware attacks.

Social Engineering:

This is the use of persuasive techniques and tactics to obtain or compromise information about you, your organization, or its computer systems for the attacker's financial gain. The methods might be quite sophisticated and manipulative.

One common form of social engineering is phishing,[2] in which e-mail is used to dupe individuals into providing personal information. Phishing attempts usually are conducted against large numbers of users, hoping to hook some of them into clicking on a malicious link or sharing sensitive personal information such as passwords, payroll information, or other financial data. By contrast, spear phishing is, as the name suggests, a more targeted approach.

In spear phishing, the attacker may use information about you or your organization to craft a message that seems quite plausible. It may even appear to be coming from someone in your educational institution and may be using a legitimate account that had been hacked to convince you to give up valuable personal information for the attacker's financial gain.

It cannot be stressed enough: review your e-mails carefully before responding, use only approved devices, and remain in the bounds of any Web surfing consistent with your educational institution's policies. In addition:

- No matter who is asking or how dire the request, *never* provide sensitive personal information, including financial information, Social Security numbers, or passwords, via e-mail.
- If you are providing sensitive information on a Web page, check the website URL. Are there typographical errors? Were you expecting it to be a .com domain, but it's a .net domain? These are signs that you may not be on a legitimate website. *Never* submit personal information unless you are certain that the site is valid and secure.
- If in doubt about any request, consult with your technology team to confirm that the request is legitimate before responding.

1. Verizon, 2018 Data Breach Investigations Report. https://www.verizonenterprise.com/resources/reports/rp_DBIR _2018_Report_execsummary_en_xg.pdf.
2. U.S. Computer Emergency Readiness Team, "Security Tip ST04-014: Avoiding Social Engineering and Phishing Attacks," 2018. https://www.us-cert.gov/ncas/tips/ST04-014.

Being security conscious helps prevent not just the tangible harms that can result when data such as a Social Security numbers, financial data, health information, or similarly sensitive data get into the hands of hackers, but the immeasurable harm that can result when we break trust with our students, parents, and colleagues, who are relying on you to do your part to handle their information carefully.

You can upgrade your data protection behaviors and make them current with the fundamental requirements for managing the data in your care in a few simple steps. In fact, we can take excerpts from the Federal Trade Commission guide to implementing reasonable security standards[11] and boil them down to ideas you can apply in your daily work. In combination, these behaviors will help improve the security profile of your educational institution, and in turn, better protect the security of your and your students' information.

In these concepts you'll recognize some of the Fair Information Practice Principles that we discussed in chapter 3.

Table 11.2.   Reasonable Security

Reasonable Security	Action Steps
1. Start with security. • Don't collect data you don't need. • Delete personal information when no longer needed. • Don't use personal information when it's not necessary.	Limit your access to student personal information to only what is essential to your work. Also ensure that the technologies you bring into the classroom only collect the minimally required personal information from and about your students. With guidance from your educational institution, ensure that appropriate contracts with any technology provider limit its use of student personal information to the legitimate educational purpose. Work with your technology team to ensure that you know how to securely delete data in all media formats when you no longer need it.
2. Control access to data sensibly. • Restrict access to sensitive data. • Limit administrative access to systems.	As discussed in the review of FERPA, only access student personal information in which you have a legitimate educational interest. Don't share data with other employees or technology providers unless you are authorized to do so. Although restricting access to systems may be the work of your technology team, you can support it by ensuring that you only request access to systems you require in order to perform in your role.

Reasonable Security	Action Steps

3. Require secure passwords and authentication.
 	
  • Insist on complex and unique passwords.
  • Store passwords securely.
  • Guard against brute force attacks.
  • Protect against authentication bypass.
	The most commonly used passwords also are the easiest for hackers to crack, and they often are looking for the path of least resistance. Don't open the door to your machine and maybe the network by using a simple password. Create a complex, unique password for each system you access.
	
	How? Make them long; use combinations of letters, numbers, and symbols; and avoid common words and phrases. Of course, doing that well means they may be difficult to remember. Put your memory techniques to work. Use mnemonics or the person-action-object technique and create passphrases. Also consult with your technology team about the possibility of using an approved password manager.
	
	Protect your passwords the way you do the contents of your wallet or the keys to your house. You wouldn't leave those items out on your desk, or anywhere in the open. You most likely keep them secured at all times. Do the same with your passwords. *They are that valuable.* Leaving them exposed puts you, your colleagues, and your students at risk. It also sends a message to your students that you are not as tech-savvy as you may want them to believe.
	
	Students have been arrested for taking advantage of visible passwords. Don't let them be tempted into what may become criminal behavior. Instead, model good security practices and keep your passwords out of sight.

4. Secure remote access to your network.
 	
  • Ensure endpoint security.
  • Put sensible access limits in place.
	Does your technology team require use of VPN and multifactor authentication to access education institution systems? Do not attempt to bypass those controls. They are there to help keep the network secure from intruders.
	
	Do not ever access your education institution systems or work from unsecure Wi-Fi, which can open your devices to intruders as described above.

(continued)

Table 11.2. *(continued)*

Reasonable Security	*Action Steps*
5. Secure paper, physical media, and devices. • Securely store sensitive files. • Protect devices that process personal information. • Keep safety standards in place when data is en route. • Dispose of sensitive data securely.	Follow your educational institution's policies related to where and how student personal information may be stored. Do not transmit student personal information through unsecured or unapproved systems. Secure your devices physically and technically. Keep them locked, protected by complex, unique passwords when not in use. If personal devices are permitted on your educational institution's network, adhere to the required security standards, such as up-to-date antivirus software, firewalls, and routine system updates, to maintain security. If personal devices are not permitted, don't compromise the security of the institution by ignoring the rules. Consult with your technology team for proper procedures to delete or destroy personal student information when no longer needed.

The process of changing behavior is not easy. However, often resistance to change takes more energy than the change itself. Start engaging in good fundamental security behavior today. In a very short time, you'll find yourself slipping easily into the routine of practicing strong security skills and will have made a tremendous impact in the security of your entire organization.

Perhaps you already are doing your part to protect the security of student data. In that case, you can be a great partner to your technology team and educational institution's leadership by championing better security practices among your colleagues. Bring your data champion behaviors to the forefront and take on a leadership role in your organization to help reduce risk to the organization, your students, and yourself.

NOTES AND NEXT STEPS

1. Refresh your security practices. Are you practicing good data security hygiene, including the use of complex, unique passwords; using multifactor authentication wherever available; securing your devices when

unattended; scrutinizing e-mails carefully before responding or clicking on links; respecting the limitations your educational institution places on software that can be on devices run on the network; and always using secure Wi-Fi for work purposes?

2. Are you protecting your students from making bad security decisions? Do you keep your passwords stored securely, out of reach of their roving eyes and curious minds?

3. What security behaviors do you expect of your students that would be worth sharing with parents? How can you partner to create a holistic eco-system where security is top of mind, when the device is being used both in the classroom and at home?

Chapter Twelve

All Hands: Building a Partnership with Your Technology Team

One of the next steps in the process is to ensure that you're not alone in the work of protecting student data privacy. Perhaps you already have a strong, positive, and collaborative relationship with your technology team. Or perhaps you've sometimes looked at them as the team that says "no" a lot, or you tend to believe that they keep you from leveraging technology in the way that you feel is most beneficial to your students.

The relationship between technology teams and educators often involves unnecessary friction. It is far too common to hear from educators that technology teams are "stifling innovation" by not permitting educators to bring certain technologies into the classroom. Equally common are technology teams expressing concern that teachers are exhibiting behaviors that put the students' personal information at risk.

The truth is that your technology team is not really in the business of standing in your way or saying no. They are very much in the business of protecting you, your students, and the educational institution from unnecessary privacy and security risk. However, often the real disconnect is in the ways you and they express concerns about data privacy and security. Clearly it is a problem, and it appears to be one of language, context, and alignment. With that comes misunderstanding that can prevent a strong partnership from forming.

Your technology team is dedicated to helping ensure that you have what you need to operate properly and safely. They may seem to be in the way or obstructing your work. Perhaps their approach is steeped in technical jargon, security acronyms, and a general sense that the sky could fall at any moment. Perhaps the sky over all things data security truly looks a bit wobbly in your educational institution, but if not, allow me to translate: they're there to protect you; perhaps they are just speaking the language of information security, not change management.

Let's first consider what the technology team does to try to better understand some of their goals. By doing so, it is likely that you'll find a smoother, solutions-oriented path to your classroom technology plans.

To date, the responsibility for protecting the privacy of student data commonly has been put in the hands of your technology team, be it an IT department, a security team, or a chief technology officer and privacy officer rolled into one. This individual or team usually has been tasked with the extraordinary work of not just ensuring that the technology functions as expected, but also of building and maintaining the technology infrastructure and ensuring that it remains secure while supporting sometimes tens of thousands of devices. To provide some context for that, it is more than many major companies have to contend with.

Educational institutions are a known ecosystem for bad actors wanting access to valuable data, and the work of keeping them out is extraordinarily complex. It involves ensuring that the network was built properly, embedded with what the Federal Trade Commission refers to as "reasonable security,"[1] and going beyond to align with a variety of nationally recognized frameworks.[2]

It requires ensuring that the technology remains up to date with the capacity to deal with the modern threat environment, continuously monitoring for such threats and interpreting the alerts that arise to separate the innocuous noise from the truly suspicious activity, identifying and assessing vulnerabilities, managing capacity needs for ever-increasing volumes of devices, and developing the policies and processes to keep your and your students' personal information secure.

The biggest threat to institution security is often not the outside actors but the people who operate on a network. In schools, this is sometimes every employee and student who uses a device. Every single piece of software downloaded onto such a device and every website accessed on it is a potential risk.

Your technology team often is responsible for deciding which sites and software to permit, which to block and which to open up perhaps only to you and not your students, based on the threat profile, network capabilities, district requirements, and CIPA requirements. Skirting any of these could compromise the security of the entire network.

In addition, as we've noted, people make mistakes. We click on links we're not supposed to. We are led to believe that an e-mail is coming to us from a supervisor when it's simply a good imitation from an outside party looking to cause havoc or steal information. And we sometimes don't listen to the warnings that tell us to create strong passwords, to not reuse our passwords, and to not use the same password for all of the systems we access. Your technology team often is tasked with trying to anticipate, stifle, and defend against all of the consequences of our very human behavior.

Their job is not to stand in the way of innovation or to interfere with teaching plans. However, the only way forward is to work together to ensure that your teaching goals are accomplished within the framework of a safe, secure environment.

That likely will mean that you're not permitted to use every piece of technology you want. However, your new understanding of the legal requirements and the challenges of securing a network may help you better understand why the educational institution policies are in place, and that maintaining strong privacy and security standards is critical for the protection of your and your students' information.

Support building a constructive partnership with your technology team where both of your voices are at the table, collaborating on solutions where they can be found.

As an educator, your voice is imperative to ensure that positive, productive, and responsible uses of student data are supported by the data protection policies and practices. Your work depends on your access to and use of a large array of student data. Do you fully understand why certain data privacy policies and processes are in place, and can you properly implement them? If not, consider working with your technology team to build a shared understanding of the requirements.

Everyone who accesses, handles, shares, or works with student data has a role to play in ensuring that the data remains protected in accordance with educational institution policies. It works best when it is a partnership between teams that are aligned around the goals of supporting positive and effective uses of the data under the direction of leadership and the processes that steer the organization away from risk.

The more you know about why the policies are in place, the better equipped you will be to articulate your data needs clearly and in a manner that is aligned with the data protection frameworks. If you believe adjustments need to be made, how can you best advocate for use of student data in a manner that is also palatable from a privacy and security perspective? How can you demonstrate better practices in protecting student data to help facilitate your use of that data?

Let's consider how you might initiate a new dynamic that is more collaborative and productive:

First, begin by reviewing your educational institution's data privacy policies. How do they reflect the legal requirements, your institution's standards, and what you know about parent expectations? Do you have questions about how to apply them to your work? Are there areas where you might need to make adjustments to your current practices?

If that's the case, even if you find the adjustments to be challenging, appreciate that the policies are in place for good reason, usually related to legal compliance as interpreted by your educational institution and protecting you and your students.

Second, create your own mission-driven statement about how you will and won't use student data. Given what you know about your educational institution's definition of legitimate educational purpose for which you may access and use personal student information, consider how you might connect that purpose to the institution's larger mission or vision.

How does the articulated legitimate educational interest in student data help your institution fulfill its mission or vision? What are the effective uses of data that support student success, development of comprehensive and balanced instruction, and help prepare students for the future? How does that shape how you might access and use personal information? Does that align with the existing data-protection policies and processes in place in your institution? Does it align with the legal requirements? If not, what changes need to be made to your practices to create alignment?

The work of protecting student data privacy is a very human endeavor. The more you and your technology team can approach the work from a collaborative point of view, the more you will be able to develop the processes that permit seamless, robust use of technology and student data in a manner that keeps the risk profile of the educational institution low but maximizes the efficacy of your data use.

Third, restart the conversation by letting your technology team know that you're more educated about the ecosystem that impacts the privacy of student data. Create an opportunity to explore existing educational institution data privacy policies together to establish a shared understanding of why they are in place. Lay the foundation for collaborating to update any untenable procedures while still accomplishing the policy goals or to develop new procedures to improve current practices.

Fourth, partner with your technology team to come up with a procedure that will better ensure that the technology you bring into the classroom is configured to comply with the legal requirements and your educational institution's policies to adequately and appropriately protect student data privacy. Establish a new partnership where you can work together to assess new technologies that you may hear about at conferences or read about in the press before bringing them into the classroom.

Fifth, understand that, despite best intentions, sometimes the answer may still be "no." Even so, the reason for that answer should be clear. It may be that the technology can't be used legally with student data, or can't be used legally with students of certain ages. It may also be that the technology provider's data privacy practices are not adequate to protect student personal information in accordance with educational institution's policy, or that adding the technology to the institution's network will jeopardize security.

Building a more collaborative relationship with your technology team will help ensure that you're given a clearer rationale and may position you to be the first to know if the technology team can identify a suitable replacement or a way to alleviate the concerns.

NOTES AND NEXT STEPS

1. Protecting student data privacy is a multi-stakeholder endeavor, and it doesn't happen without your involvement. How can you encourage a more collaborative approach to the work? What do you need from your technology team to improve your data protection practices?
2. What data protection practices can you now teach your students? How can they collaborate with you to improve the data protection environment in your classroom?
3. Review your educational institution's acceptable or responsible use policy. Are there pieces of it you can tie to the work your technology team does that also support your technology use?

Chapter Thirteen

Students and Parents

You are a role model for your students. You know this, but do you consider it when it comes to your technology practices? Your students notice everything about you: when you change your hair, that new tie you started wearing, what makes you laugh in class, if you never laugh in class.

Even when they are not paying attention, your students are absorbing the tone and tenor of the environment. They know you as you present yourself in the classroom almost as well as you know them: your moods, your expectations, what makes you laugh, what displeases you. We can even say that, most of the time, they want to make you proud. You have a unique and powerful opportunity to influence how they start to think about protecting the privacy of their personal information.

What are they learning from you about how to protect their privacy? In their digital citizenship lessons, you may be teaching them online etiquette and how to surf the internet safely. Certainly, cyberbullying is a big topic for many classrooms, and helping students deal with the very real challenges of growing up online, out loud, as they do.

You likely cover the importance of thinking before posting online, how to protect their online reputation, what your students should do if they see something online that makes them uncomfortable, and more. It's possible that your lesson plans also include modules on privacy and security behaviors, and perhaps you've included digital literacy lessons as well.

All of this is incredibly important in helping guide students to be safe online, to use technology responsibly, and to make better decisions about their online behavior. However, it usually doesn't go far enough in preparing students to make smart decisions about their privacy now or in the future. To truly prepare your students for the world, take whatever opportunities you can to reinforce that personal privacy includes privacy of the information they share through their devices.

Creating lesson plans focused specifically on privacy and security would be a valuable addition to the modern education. However, I appreciate that may not be terribly realistic, given the sheer volume of other education priorities. Short of delivering on a curriculum dedicated to data privacy and security, how do you model lessons on data privacy in your daily actions?

As you well know, students watch and learn. They soak up life lessons from everyone around them. As an educator, you have a tremendously valuable opportunity to begin teaching students that privacy matters, or at the least, that it's something to consider actively. The ways in which you behave to protect student data often are visible in your classroom, and what is visible can be modeled. You know that your students are watching you. Do you demonstrate good data privacy behaviors in the classroom as you interact with technology?

The care you take to secure your computer whenever you leave the classroom. The way in which you return test papers, with the grades facing down so that students can't see each other's results. The fact that your students never know where your passwords are kept. The private conversations you have with students about their need for improvement, out of earshot of others. All of these behaviors and more communicate to them that their privacy is important—and that protecting it is worthwhile.

What would it take for you to add to that repertoire? The next time you introduce a new technology into the classroom, would it be easy to point out where students can find a link to the privacy policy? This is not about asking them to read it, but simply noting that it exists and where it can be found. What would it mean to explain to students the process you go through to choose new technologies?

Simply begin by being mindful about the steps you take to protect student data privacy and make note of them. In whatever way you can manage, start showing your students that being thoughtful about protecting their privacy is important. It is a critical lesson they need, and your use of technology in the classroom is a perfect teaching opportunity. Share what you know with your students.

Here are a few behaviors you can model for your students without the need to create a special lesson plan. Let your students see you in action around these simple steps:

- Don't store your passwords on or near the computer or in the desk. Students should believe that you have memorized all of your passwords (and you should do so). Talk to your technology team about an approved password manager program if you have trouble with that, but let your students see that you treat that password like the rare and valuable item that it is, and keep it out of sight.

- Lock your computer whenever you leave the classroom. Don't ever leave it unattended and unlocked.
- When using a new app or website in the classroom, point out where the link to the privacy policy can be found and explain its purpose. Take at least one opportunity to explain what you or others in your educational institution do to review technology products for privacy and security before asking students to use it. Don't lead your students to believe that the process for using a new technology product is simply to "download and go," without first considering data privacy.
- If your educational institution allows the use of portable storage devices, ensure that they are always secure, never out on a desktop or elsewhere.
- When you post grades, ensure that you are not revealing a student identifier the whole class will know. Each student should only know his or her results. Point out this practice to your students so they see the care you are taking with their privacy.
- Ensure that the projects you assign incorporate strong privacy practices by avoiding asking students to share their personal information or conduct research on platforms that might compromise their privacy.

What other things can you do that simply model good data privacy practices for your own information and your students' information? Small actions can make a difference, especially when it is something that your students may not be learning from anyone else.

Working with Parents

No doubt teachers are the first source of truth about the educational institution for parents. You are their touchstone for information about their child and their child's academic, social, and emotional progress in school. They look to you to care for and about their child and to guide their child through the academic careers.

You are the face of your educational institution and the very representation of the standard of care that it provides to each child. Parents place a tremendous amount of trust in you to educate and care for and about their child. They often look to you for answers.

When it comes to student data privacy and use of technology in the classroom, it's difficult to overstate the level of concern many parents have. For many educational institutions, parental concerns about use of technology in the classroom are real and palpable, and they can make adopting technologies challenging for the institution.

Perhaps you've heard questions from parents worried about how much time their child spends in front of a screen, or asking to opt their child out from use of certain classroom technologies for fear that the technology provider is not up to the task of properly protecting their child's personal information. Or perhaps you've heard questions about whether the child's poor performance, in the hands of a technology provider, might someday be used to limit future opportunities.

If you haven't heard questions from parents about classroom technologies or student data privacy yet, you probably soon will. Technology is complex and ever changing, and it's easy for parents to feel that it is simply taking over their child's life. Rightly or wrongly, they often look to their educational institutions to have the answers.

Thankfully, as educators, you know that the antidote to fear often is knowledge. It's one reason why it's imperative that you are able to answer their questions. In fact, you can likely stave off most questions in the first place with proactive leadership as you engage with parents of your students.

You don't need to become a technology expert in order to respond well to their questions and attempt to address their fears with information about your educational institution's technology program, including your use of technology in the classroom.

Taking the uncertainty out of the equation for parents will create a climate that fosters sensible conversation about technology use based on facts, not fear.

You already work with many parents, sharing information about the lessons you plan to impart, your expectations for the class, and how their child is progressing. Adding a thoughtful discussion about your use of technology in the classroom is an important part of that conversation. Also consider whether you have opportunities to show parents the technology that their child will be using in the classroom. All of these steps can help demystify the modern classroom, which will pave the way for less friction during your school year.

What, specifically, do parents want to hear from you? What can you tell them that will help them view your technology program with confidence? It begins with the fundamentals. To the extent possible, work with your leadership to develop materials that inform parents about the following:[1]

Why does your educational institution collect student data?

The answer seems obvious to you, but to many parents, the volume of student data collected in schools is *exponentially* more than it was when they were students. That may or may not be the case, but certainly more data is being collected than ever before. That's often the result of additional educational institution services that have evolved to address modern-day issues that surface in schools, as well as the use of technology, which results in collection of additional data, often passively.

What can you tell parents about why your educational institution collects the information it does? What is required by the state, and how do technology providers use the information they receive to benefit students? If information is shared for research purposes, how might the results or beneficial outcomes be shared with parents?

What positive uses of student data facilitate a better educational experience? How does collection and use of student data help fulfill the educational institution's mission and vision?

Why is technology used in the classroom?

Again, that may seem like a very simple question, but for parents who are concerned about data collection, protection, screen time, and that technology may be used in a way that replaces your guidance and expertise, it's a question that demands an answer. What can you tell parents about why you use certain technologies in the classroom? How can you best articulate the way you leverage technology and weave it into the curriculum to support your teaching goals? Perhaps most important, how does the use of technology benefit each student?

How does your educational institution ensure that student data is protected, even when shared with technology providers?

This is often the crux of the matter. It may be the most challenging question for you to answer if you don't yet have visibility into your educational institution's data protection program. Parents want to know more about the work you do to protect the privacy of their children's personal information beyond simply noting that the institution complies with the laws.

This is another area where a partnership with your technology team can help you support parents. Work together with them to develop an answer to this question that addresses protections in place for the educational institution. In addition, be able to explain how the technologies you bring into the classroom are assessed to ensure that:

- Each piece of technology used in the classroom has a defined curriculum purpose and goal;
- The technology is age appropriate for your students;
- The technology providers offer adequate and appropriate protections for student data that meet the legal requirements as well as educational institution policies for protecting student data privacy, and that is articulated in a contractual agreement, be it the technology provider's standard terms or the educational institution's contract;
- Only the minimally required personal information necessary to leverage the product in the classroom is shared with any technology provider;
- The educational institution maintains direct control over the personal student information in the education record, even when it is shared with the technology provider, and what that direct control generally entails;
- A reminder of their data rights or where they can go to learn more information about their data rights.

Other commonly asked questions from parents include:

- Is each piece of technology used in the classroom mandatory?
- How much time does my child spend on screens in the classroom? What is the quality of that screen time?
- How do you ensure that technology providers delete my child's personal information when they're finished using the product?
- What steps are in place to ensure that school employees and technology providers are only using my child's personal information for educational purposes?
- How can I access my child's education record?

If you're unsure of the answers to any of these questions, visit with your educational institution leadership or technology team to start working on a plan to map out the responses.

As the face of the educational institution for parents, being able to provide them with this information will reassure them of your capabilities and competencies. It also will help to ensure that when parents do have questions or objections to use of technology in the classroom, you will be prepared for a fact-based discussion.

You may never convince all of the parents that the use of technology and associated data collection is beneficial. However, your ability to convey the fundamentals about data collection, use, and protection to parents in a well-informed conversation about the concerns will build trust, which will go a long way toward facilitating reasonable dialogue.

NOTES AND NEXT STEPS

1. Leverage what you know, as well as information from your technology team and educational institution leadership so you are empowered to articulate how data collection benefits each student.
2. Model appropriate data privacy behaviors in the classroom, and show your students simple steps you take to protect their privacy, in turn reinforcing for them that information about them is personal and worth protecting.
3. Be able to articulate how and why you use technology in the classroom, how each student benefits from that technology use, and how you and your educational institution work to ensure that student data privacy is protected, including the steps you take specifically to manage your privacy and security responsibilities around the technology you bring into the classroom.

Epilogue

Protecting the privacy of student data is not an easy task, nor is it something that can be done only by one individual following a few simple rules. It requires thinking about data as a valuable asset and treating it as such, in alignment with complex legal and education institution requirements. It also requires doing this work in close partnership with all other stakeholders, following the seasoned guidance of your leadership and technology teams while maintaining what you need to keep your focus on your critical work.

Doing it well can be a massive organizational undertaking, made all the more challenging because many of the policies and procedures that now govern sensible student data protection behaviors and manage the inherent risks weren't in place before technology was brought into the classroom.

The process of catching up to the new normal can be challenging, but everyone in the organization needs to be aligned around the work. To be successful requires that all stakeholders be invested in making the sometimes small but meaningful behavioral adjustments that evolve existing practices to the level that respects privacy of the students.

Your work is pivotal to success for the education institution and the students you support.

Changing our behavior is never easy, and it's often made even more challenging when the results of our behavior change are intangible, as it sometimes is with privacy behavior.

For example, you won't know if you have prevented a security breach by not posting your password on your laptop. However, you can be certain that you have created risk by making it available.

Other certainties you can rely on are that by not unnecessarily accessing or sharing student personal information, you are helping your organization meet its legal responsibilities, and that by facilitating or contributing to a privacy and security assessment of classroom technologies before introducing them to students, you are helping to ensure that the products they use are designed to safely meet your learning goals for them.

You already have the goals in place: you want your students to be nothing less than prepared for their futures. You guide them to be leaders, to make responsible and well-reasoned decisions, to be critical thinkers, skilled communicators, and productive contributors to society. You transform their lives.

Continue on that path by embracing the responsibility of helping to protect your students' privacy. As you improve your practices in this area, pass what you know on to your students. In doing so, you'll be a savvier educator, better-positioned to build stronger partnerships with your education institution leadership, technology teams and parents around your use of technology in the classroom. You'll also be teaching your students a critical skill for navigating the modern world: empowerment over their privacy.

Take heart in knowing that the lessons you incorporate into your teaching practice about the fundamentals of data privacy and technology will not change no matter what the device, program or product. The technology may change, but the fundamental concepts that govern solid privacy and security will remain for decades to come. This will serve you well in protecting your students' privacy and your own.

It is unfortunate that learning how to properly manage your data privacy responsibilities has to compete with so many other priorities. However, that is the very real nature of the modern education institution, which is a microcosm of societal issues compressed into a small space and being played out on a daily basis. And those issues are often much closer to survival needs than data privacy.

It is also unfortunate that data privacy doesn't come neatly packaged in a few short steps that will keep everything secure. However, that is also the very real nature of a discipline that is contextual and focused on human behavior.

I encourage you to make small, incremental changes that leverage what you've learned here, and build from there, moving towards ever-stronger privacy practices over time.

Review the data protection policies and processes that exist in your education institution and bring them to life in a more deliberate fashion. Be a champion to your colleagues and share your knowledge. Build a stronger, more collaborative partnership with your technology team and work together to improve the privacy ecosystem that you work in. Be a role model for your students and encourage the designers, coders and builders of tomorrow to think about the responsibility that comes with technology.

Most importantly, empower your students and instill in them the education they need to be able to make the smart, deliberate choices about their privacy and about how to better navigate their technology-infused futures.

Notes

CHAPTER ONE: WHAT IS DATA PRIVACY AND WHY DOES IT MATTER?

1. Teach Tomorrow, "Continuing Education for Teachers," https://www.teach tomorrow.org/continuing-education-for-teachers/.
2. Ponemon Institute Research Report, "2017 Cost of a Data Breach Study." Ponemon Institute, June 2017.
3. Danah Boyd, *It's Complicated: The Social Lives of Networked Teens* (New Haven, CT: Yale University Press, 2014).

CHAPTER TWO: HOW DID WE GET HERE?

1. Monica Butler, Patrick McCormick, and Mikaela Pitcam, "The Legacy of InBloom," Data & Society, 2017. https://datasociety.net/pubs/ecl/InBloom_feb _2017.pdf.
2. Rachel Abrams, "Target to Pay $18.5 Million to 47 States in Security Breach Settlement," *New York Times*, 2017. https://www.nytimes.com/2017/05/23/business/ target-security-breach-settlement.html.
3. Natasha.Singer, "Deciding Who Sees Student Data," *New York Times*, 2013. http://www.nytimes.com/2013/10/06/business/deciding-who-sees-students-data .html. "Students are currently subject to more forms of tracking and monitoring than ever before," Khaliah Barnes, a lawyer at the Electronic Privacy Information Center in Washington who appeared via video conferencing, told the room packed with parents. "While we understand the value of data for promoting and evaluating personalized learning, there are too few safeguards for the amount of data collected and transmitted from schools to private companies."

4. Senator Edward J, Markey, 2013. https://www.markey.senate.gov/documents/2013-10-22_FERPA.pdf.

5. Secretary Arne Duncan, 2014. https://www.markey.senate.gov/documents/2014-01-10_Education_Privacy.pdf.

6. Joel Reidenberg, N. Cameron Russell, Jordan Kovnot, Thomas B. Norton, Ryan Cloutier, and Daniela Alvarado, "Privacy and Cloud Computing in Public Schools," *Center on Law and Information Policy*, book 2, 2013. http://ir.lawnet.fordham.edu/clip/2http://ir.lawnet.fordham.edu/cgi/viewcontent.cgi?article=1001&context=clip.

7. Ibid.

8. Data Quality Campaign. "Complying with FERPA and Other Federal Privacy and Security Laws and Maximizing Appropriate Data Use," 2013. https://dataqualitycampaign.org/resource/complying-ferpa-federal-privacy-security-laws-maximizing-appropriate-data-use/. "Utah Teachers Value, Use and Need Data," 2018. https://dataqualitycampaign.org/resource/utah-teachers-value-use-and-need-data/.

9. *Education Week*, "Exit Strategy: State Lawmakers Consider Dropping Common Core." https://www.edweek.org/ew/section/multimedia/anti-cc-bill.html.

10. Emma Brown, "Debate over Test Security vs. Student Privacy Rages in the Age of Social Media," *Washington Post*, 2015. https://www.washingtonpost.com/local/education/debate-over-test-security-vs-student-privacy-rages-in-the-age-of-social-media/2015/03/23/bbac030a-cf0c-11e4-a2a7-9517a3a70506_story.html?utm_term=.0bc6a2849019; and The Pew Charitable Trusts, "Common Core Sparks Flood of Legislation," 2014. https://www.pewtrusts.org/en/research-and-analysis/blogs/stateline/2014/06/12/common-core-sparks-flood-of-legislation.

11. Data Quality Campaign, "Student Data Privacy Legislation. What Happened in 2015 and What is Next?" https://2pido73em67o3eytaq1cp8au-wpengine.netdna-ssl.com/wp-content/uploads/2016/03/DQC-Student-Data-Laws-2015-Sept23.pdf.

CHAPTER THREE: WHAT INFORMATION ARE WE TRYING TO PROTECT?

1. "Family Educational Rights and Privacy Act," 20 U.S.C. § 1232g; 34 CFR Part 99.

CHAPTER FOUR: KEY PRIVACY CONCEPTS

1. Department of Homeland Security, "Fair Information Practice Principles." https://www.dhs.gov/publication/fair-information-practice-principles-fipps; and Pam Dixon, World Privacy Forum, "A Brief Introduction to Fair Information Practices." https://www.worldprivacyforum.org/2008/01/report-a-brief-introduction-to-fair-information-practices/.

CHAPTER FIVE: FAMILY EDUCATIONAL RIGHTS AND PRIVACY ACT

1. "Family Educational Rights and Privacy Act," 20 U.S.C. § 1232g; 34 CFR Part 99.

2. "Family Educational Rights and Privacy Act," 20 U.S.C. § 1232g; 34 CFR Part 99.

3. National Center for Education Statistics, "Defining 'Legitimate Educational Interest.'" https://nces.ed.gov/pubs2004/privacy/section_4b.asp.

4. U.S. Department of Education Privacy Technical Assistance Center and the Family Policy Compliance Office, "Data De-identification: An Overview of the Basic Terms." https://studentprivacy.ed.gov/sites/default/files/resource_document/file/data_deidentification_terms_0.pdf.

5. General Education Provisions Act. https://legcounsel.house.gov/Comps/General%20Education%20Provisions%20Act.pdf.

CHAPTER SIX: STILL MORE LAWS

1. "Protection of Pupil Rights Amendment," 20 U.S.C. § 1232h (2000 & Supp. IV 2004). http://familypolicy.ed.gov/content/ppra-requirements.

2. Data Quality Campaign, "Education Data Legislation Review: 2017 State Activity." https://dataqualitycampaign.org/resource/2017-education-data-legislation/.

3. Student Online Privacy Protection Act. https://leginfo.legislature.ca.gov/faces/billNavClient.xhtml?bill_id=201320140SB1177.

4. Student Online Privacy Protection Act. https://leginfo.legislature.ca.gov/faces/billNavClient.xhtml?bill_id=201320140SB1177.

5. New York State Education Law Section 2D. http://public.leginfo.state.ny.us/lawssrch.cgi?NVLWO.

6. 16 CFR Part 312, Children's Online Privacy Protection Rule. https://www.ecfr.gov/cgi-bin/text-idx?SID=4939e77c77a1a1a08c1cbf905fc4b409&node=16%3A1.0.1.3.36&rgn=div5.

7. Bills have been proposed in Congress to add protections to COPPA for individuals ages thirteen to sixteen; in the EU, under the General Data Protection Regulation (GDPR) the age of a child for the purpose of being able to provide consent for privacy purposes varies by country. However, at the time of publication of this book, COPPA remains a U.S. law that protects the privacy of personal information collected online from children under the age of thirteen.

8. Do Not Track Kids Act. https://www.markey.senate.gov/imo/media/doc/Do%20Not%20Track%20Kids%20Act.pdf.

9. Federal Trade Commission, "Comply with COPPA: Frequently Asked Questions." https://www.ftc.gov/tips-advice/business-center/guidance/complying-coppa-frequently-asked-questions#Schools.

10. Federal Trade Commission, "Comply with COPPA: Frequently Asked Questions." https://www.ftc.gov/tips-advice/business-center/guidance/complying-coppa-frequently-asked-questions#COPPA Enforcement.

11. Federal Communications Commission, "Children's Internet Protection Act Consumer Guide." https://www.fcc.gov/consumers/guides/childrens-internet-protection-act.

12. U.S. Department of Agriculture Food and Nutrition Service, National Student Lunch Act. https://www.fns.usda.gov/nslp/history_5.

13. U.S. Department of Health and Human Services, U.S. Department of Education, "Joint Guidance on the Application of the Family Educational Rights and Privacy Act (FERPA) and the Health Insurance Portability and Accountability Act of 1996 (HIPAA) to Student Health Records," November 2008. https://www2.ed.gov/policy/gen/guid/fpco/doc/ferpa-hipaa-guidance.pdf.

CHAPTER SEVEN: BRINGING TECHNOLOGY INTO THE CLASSROOM

1. Federal Trade Commission. "Comply with COPPA: Frequently Asked Questions." https://www.ftc.gov/tips-advice/business-center/guidance/complying-coppa-frequently-asked-questions#COPPA Enforcement.

CHAPTER ELEVEN: SECURITY SIMPLIFIED

1. Dillon Tabish, "Authorities: Overseas Hackers Seeking to Extort Community with Cyber Threats," *Flathead Beacon*, 2017. https://flatheadbeacon.com/2017/09/18/authorities-overseas-hackers-seeking-extort-community-cyber-threats/.

2. Peter Friesen and Gwen Florio, "Ransom Letter from Flathead County Cyber Attackers Reveals Motive," *Missoulian*, 2017. https://missoulian.com/news/local/ransom-letter-from-flathead-county-cyber-attackers-details-motive/article_ba037e6f-2267-5db3-95f2-ddbb20cba6a3.html.

3. Benjamin Herold, "They Hacked Their School District When They Were 12. The Adults Are Still Trying to Catch Up," *Education Week*, 2018. https://www.edweek.org/ew/articles/2018/11/07/they-hacked-their-school-district-when-they.html.

4. Jennifer Chambers, "Student Hacker Shows Holes in K–12 Cybersecurity," *Detroit News*, 2018. https://www.detroitnews.com/story/news/education/2018/10/03/rochester-hills-student-hacking/1369297002/.

5. Ese Olumhense, "Chicago Public Schools Mistakenly Emails Private Data of Thousands of Students, Including Names, Phone Numbers," *Chicago Tribune*, 2018. https://www.chicagotribune.com/news/local/breaking/ct-met-chicago-public-schools-data-breach-20180616-story.html.

6. Matt Masterson, "CPS: Ousted Ogden Principal Exposed Private Student Info in New Data Breach," *WTTW*, 2018. https://news.wttw.com/2018/12/28/cps-ousted -ogden-principal-exposed-private-student-info-new-data-breach.

7. Lindsey O'Donnell, "San Diego School District Data Breach Hits 500k Students," *Threatpost*, 2018. https://threatpost.com/san-diego-school-district-data -breach-hits-500k-students/140366/.

8. "Read: SDUSD Letter Notifying Families of Data Breach," *Fox 5 San Diego*, 2018. https://fox5sandiego.com/2018/12/21/read-sdusd-letter-notifying-families-of -data-breach/.

9. Verizon, 2018 Data Breach Investigations Report. https://www.verizon enterprise.com/resources/reports/rp_DBIR_2018_Report_execsummary_en_xg.pdf.

10. House Committee on Education and the Workforce, "Protecting Privacy, Promoting Data Security," May 17, 2018. https://www.youtube.com/watch ?v=FUPjfdwG8F8.

11. Federal Trade Commission, "Start with Security." https://www.ftc.gov/ system/files/documents/plain-language/pdf0205-startwithsecurity.pdf; Information Systems Audit and Controls Association (ISACA), http://www.isaca.org/cobit/pages/ default.aspx; International Organization for Standardization (ISO), https://www.iso .org/home.html; National Institute of Standards and Technology (NIST), https:// www.nist.gov/; Open Web Application Security Project (OWASP), https://www .owasp.org/index.php/Main_Page.

CHAPTER TWELVE: ALL HANDS: BUILDING A PARTNERSHIP WITH YOUR TECHNOLOGY TEAM

1. Federal Trade Commission, "Start with Security." https://www.ftc.gov/system/ files/documents/plain-language/pdf0205-startwithsecurity.pdf.

2. Information Systems Audit and Controls Association (ISACA), http://www .isaca.org/cobit/pages/default.aspx; International Organization for Standardization (ISO), https://www.iso.org/home.html; National Institute of Standards and Technology (NIST), https://www.nist.gov/; Open Web Application Security Project (OWASP), https://www.owasp.org/index.php/Main_Page.

CHAPTER THIRTEEN: WORKING WITH PARENTS

1. Free infographics are available from Consortium for School Networking. http://cosn.org/ProtectingPrivacy and Data Quality Campaign and https://dataquality campaign.org/resources/.

About the Author

Photo Credit: Marj Kleinman

Linnette Attai is the founder PlayWell, LLC, a global compliance consulting firm providing strategic guidance around the complex obligations governing data privacy, marketing, safety, and content. Linnette brings more than twenty-five years of experience to the work, advising on privacy and marketing regulations, developing policy frameworks and compliant monetization models, and building organizational cultures of compliance. She also serves as virtual chief privacy officer and as General Data Protection Regulation (GDPR) data protection officer to a range of organizations. Linnette is a recognized expert in the youth and education sectors and speaks nationally on data privacy. In addition to this book, she is the author of *Student Data Privacy: Building a School Compliance Program*.

Made in United States
Orlando, FL
30 March 2022